Dr… …ein
& Collected Poems
1967–1984

LIZ LOCHHEAD

DREAMING FRANKENSTEIN

& COLLECTED POEMS 1967-1984

First published in Great Britain in 1984 by Polygon Books

This edition first published in 2003
by Polygon an imprint of Birlinn Ltd
West Newington House
10 Newington Road
Edinburgh EH9 1QS

The publisher acknowledges subsidy from the Scottish Arts Council towards the publication of this volume.

Cover design by James Hutcheson
Typeset by Koinonia, Bury, Lancashire
Printed and bound in Great Britain by Cromwell Press, Trowbridge

British Library Cataloguing in Publication Data

A catalogue record is available on request from the British Library

ISBN 0 9544075 1 2

In memory of Tarık Okyay

Contents

THE GRIMM SISTERS (1981)

ISLANDS (1978)

MEMO FOR SPRING (1972)

Foreword

It is good to have this substantial collection of Liz Lochhead's poems. Although she has become increasingly well known as a public performer of her work, and has shown her growing interest in the theatre by writing plays, her poetry is skilled and crafted and asks to be read as well as heard. Of her two main previous books, *Memo for Spring* (1972) brought a fresh and distinctive voice to everyday subjects – growing up, a carnival, a dance cloakroom, a younger sister, school prizes, a neighbour's sari, a warrant sale, being in hospital, making a phone call; *The Grimm Sisters* (1981) moved further into both narrative and character-sketch, and added a dimension taken from ballad and fairy-tale.

The present volume, with a large number of new poems, brings a range of material and confidence of tone which are most impressive. Human relationships, especially as seen from a woman's point of view, are central: attraction, pain, acceptance, loss, triumphs and deceptions, habits and surprises; always made immediate through a storyteller's concrete detail of place or voice or object or colour, remembered or imagined. The tone varies from the rueful to something very forceful and deck-clearing indeed. Darker undercurrents suggested by the book's title accompany an emerging theme of self-exploring and self-defining which makes 'Mirror's Song' a key poem: 'a woman giving birth to herself'. This is a bold, striking collection. Poetry in Scotland is evidently not lacking in health and flair.

Edwin Morgan, 1984

Preface

I am grateful to my publishers, Polygon, for keeping this book continuously in print for the last two decades and even more grateful for this chance – as we go to press with my new collection *The Colour of Black & White* – to make a new, improved edition of *Dreaming Frankenstein & Collected Poems 1967–1984*. A chance to correct the many typographical errors, to revisit my own often eccentric punctuation – different conventions *do* pertain to different poems, but these do seem to have been inconsistently applied by me – a chance to have a proper contents page and correct a glaring omission which has often discomfited me as I shuffled, in public, on a platform at a literary festival or a school, through the pages in search of a particular poem.

I have resisted – though it was often hard – the desire to edit, omit or rewrite my old poems, my old self or selves. I used to resent these poems being called *personal* or *confessional* and, I think, rightly, truthfully, stressed that I was writing in a consciously created *persona* and was genuinely interested in the fictional, the dramatised, the spoken voice of the character. Ah well, working through them, now, this closely, this concentratedly, they seem to me as naked and as intimate as any journal, and sometimes painfully so. I just have to hope that the test of them will say something about growing up and growing older, particularly growing up and growing older *female* in a particular time and place. And remind myself that I wrote them for the same reason as I, less prolifically, write poems now. For consolation, and for fun.

Liz Lochhead, April 2003

Acknowledgements

The author would like to thank the Scottish Arts Council, the Arts Council of Great Britain and the Canada Council for awarding her the writer-in-residence fellowships that helped to create the time to write *Dreaming Frankenstein* and *The Grimm Sisters.*

The author would like to acknowledge the following for publishing or broadcasting some of the poems that appear in *Dreaming Frankenstein*: Akros, Aquarius, BBC, Broadsheet, Cencrastus, Clanjamfrie, Cracked Looking Glass, Forum Germany, Glasgow Magazine, GUM, Poetry Australia, Thancy, This Magazine, Toronto Life, Words, Zip.

Dreaming Frankenstein (1984)

Illustration by *Lys Hansen.*

What the Pool Said, on Midsummer's Day

I've led you by my garrulous banks, babbling
on and on till – drunk on air
and sure it's only water talking –
you come at last to my silence.
Listen, I'm dark
and still and deep enough.
Even this hottest gonging sun
on this longest day
can't white me out.
What are you waiting for?
I lie here, inviting, winking you in.

The woman was easy.
Like to like, I called her, she came.
In no time I had her
out of herself, slipping on my water-stockings,
leaning into, being cupped and clasped
in my green glass bra.
But it's you I want, and you know it, man.
I watch you, stripped, knee-deep
in my shallows, telling yourself
that what makes you gasp
and balls your gut
is not my coldness but your own fear.

– Your reasonable fear,
what's true in me admits it.
(Though deeper, oh
older than any reason.)
Yes, I could
drown you, you
could foul my depths, it's not
unheard of. What's fish
in me could make flesh of you,

my wet weeds against your thigh, it
could turn nasty.
I could have you
gulping fistfuls fighting yourself
back from me.

I get darker and darker, suck harder.
On-the-brink man, you
wish I'd flash and dazzle again.
You'd make a fetish of zazzing dragonflies?
You want I should zip myself up
with the kingfisher's flightpath, be beautiful?
I say no tricks. I say just trust,
I'll soak through your skin and
slake your thirst.

I watch. You clench,
clench and come into me.

An Abortion

The first inkling I had of the beast's agony
was the something not right
of her scrabbling, scrabbling
to still not quite find
all four feet.
Sunk again, her cow-tongue lolled
then spiked the sky, she rolled
great gape-mouth, neck distended
in a Guernica of distress.
That got through to me all right
behind glass as I was
a whole flat field away.
It took an emblem-bellow
to drag me from my labour
at the barbed words on my desk top.

Close to, green foam flecked her muzzle
and drizzled between the big bared brown teeth.
Spasms, strong, primeval
as the pulsing locomotion of some
terrible underwater creature,
rippled down her flank
and her groan was the more awesome
for being drier, no louder than a cough.
When she tried to rise again
I saw it.
Membrane wrapped, the head of a calf
hung out and the wrong-looking bundle
of a knuckle. Then her rope-tail dropped
and she fell back on it, steamrollering it
under her.

When the summoned men came,
buttoning blue coveralls over
the Sunday lunches and good-suit waistcoats,
the wound string around one man's knuckles

meant business and the
curt thank-you-very-much of the other
dismissed me.

Shamed voyeur, back at my notebooks again
my peeled eyes caught the quick hoick
of the string loop, the dead thing flopping
to the grass, the cow on her knees and
up again, the men leaving, one
laughing at some punchline.

The thing is this. Left alone,
that cow licking at those lollop limbs
which had not formed properly
with her long tongue,
that strong tongue
which is a match for thistles
and salt-lick coarse as pumice stone
tenderly over and over again at
what has come out of her and she is responsible for
as if she can not believe it will not
come alive,
not if she licks long enough.

Outside she is still licking, licking
till in the blue dusk
the men in blue come back again
and she turns, goes quietly with them
as if they were policemen
and she knew exactly what she were guilty of.

1. Dreaming Frankenstein
for Lys Hansen, Jacki Parry and June Redfern

She said she
woke up with him in
her head, in her bed.
Her mother-tongue clung to her mouth's roof
in terror, dumbing her, and he came with a name
that was none of her making.

No maidservant ever
in her narrow attic, combing
out her hair in the midnight mirror
on Hallowe'en (having eaten
that egg with its yolk hollowed out
then filled with salt)
as a spell to summon up her lover
– oh never one had such success as this
she had not courted.
The amazed flesh of her
neck and shoulders nettled
at his apparition.

Later, stark staring awake to everything
(the room, the dark parquet, the white high Alps beyond)
all normal in the moonlight
and him gone, save a ton-weight sensation,
the marks fading visibly where
his buttons had bit into her and
the rough serge of his suiting had chafed her sex,
she knew – oh that was not how –
but he'd entered her utterly.

This was the penetration
of seven swallowed apple pips.
Or else he'd slipped like a silver dagger
between her ribs and healed her up secretly
again. Anyway

he was inside her
and getting him out again
would be agony fit to quarter her,
unstitching everything.

Eyes on those high peaks
in the reasonable sun of the morning,
she dressed in damped muslin
and sat down to quill and ink
and icy paper.

2. What the Creature Said

The blind man did not hate me.
I saw him through the window,
through the rippling circle my own
hot breath had melted
in the spiky flowers of the frost.

I was exhausted,
imagine it. Midwinter. Mountains.
Forest. Dragging my bad leg
over iron ground, impossible passes,
pained by that fleshwound where
that villager's silver bullet
grazed me.

There he was, bent
above the hot soup, supping
his solitude from a bone spoon.
And when my single rap
at the glass spun him full face
towards me, mild as a cat,
my heart stopped but oh
he did not flinch.

Then I saw his
milky eyes stared right through me,
unblinking, and he fumbled
oddly forward to meet me at the latch.
I lifted it and entered,
sure that I found a friend.

3. Smirnoff for Karloff

for Marilyn Bowering and Bessie Smith

So you're who's been sleeping
in my bed. Well, hello there.
Long time no see.
So you're my Big Fat Little Secret
stretched out cold,
just between you and me.

Between you and me and the bedpost
it's getting a little crowded in here.
Roll over, let me whisper sweet zeroes
in your Good Ear.
Open up your Glad Eye.
Oh my! I'm going to make you.
Going to make you sit up.
Going to make you.
Going to take you to bits.
Going to take you to the cleaners.
Going to make you look cute,
going to let you roly-pole all over me
in your funeral suit –
the one you wear to weddings. Yeah.
With the too short drainpipe trousers
with the brothelcreeper boots with the
tyre-track soles
and the squirt-in-the-eye trick carnation
in your button-hole.

You know Matron
take more than hospital corners to keep
a good man down, oh
yeah. Everything
in applepie order.
All present
and correct. Shipshape. Aye-aye.
He got all my wits around him
his extrasensory senses and his
five straight limbs.
Yes sir,
you'll be up and about again
in no time.

What wouldn't you
give to love me. An arm, and a leg?
Going to make you.
make you sit up,
sit up and beg. Hey, Mister,
Mister can your dog do tricks?
Going to make you,
going to put you to the test,
make you give your all six
nights per week and on Sundays
going to take the rest.

Sure, you can smoke in bed.
It's a free country.
Let me pour you a stiff drink.
You're shivering.
Well, you know what they say, if you
can't take the cold then get outa
the icebox. What's that?
Smirnoff?
Well, you know, Mr Karloff,
I used to think an aphrodisiac was some
kinda confused Tibetan mountain goat
with a freak-out hair-do until I
met my monster and my monster

met his maker.
Oh yeah.

That who been sleeping in my bed.
Same old surprise. Oh goody.
Long time no see.
Ain't going to let nothing come between
My monster and me.

Smuggler

for Susan Musgrave

Why she loved him, she said, was for
his black pirate's heart.
Get her, adrift in his
brass bed, half seas over, stared awake
by the match box she found last night
balanced on the bed head.
Contents: one single scarlet fingernail.

Love?
She explains it another way.
In a heatwave between the wars,
her maiden aunt once told her,
high in the Campsies (they had cycled
from Glasgow, they were fourteen, with
packed lunches in the baskets between the horns
of their handlebars) they skinnydipped and sunbathed
naked, she and her sister, and she slept.
She woke up later to a cloud and a bird like
a hawk circling and Nettie, her sister, her twin,
the one who died of TB at the time of Munich,
leant over her and bit her nipple off.

She explains it another way.

Page from a Biography

When she was seventeen she left home, secretly,
and lived rough amid the Axminster:
Became clever as Caliban at knowing the most
nourishing morsels among the jewel-berries she filched from
the chintz.
Left alone she'd sample every tipple in the drinks cupboard
(topping up the junglejuice with tapwater).
She learned to name her poison
and know her true enemies.

She'd left no note but as they
did not seem to notice she'd gone she never
heard the dee-jay appeal for her return
or at least a postcard, no need for an address,
to set their minds at rest.

As for the weasel, well there was no sign of one
and this family wasn't cocktail cabinet class
but occasionally she thought she glimpsed
something furry and honey coloured with Christknows
what kind of jaws and teeth slink behind the radiogram
and lie there limp as a draught excluder.

She poked the odd clandestine crust at it
flattering herself that Trouble was her middle name.

The People's Poet
for Edwin Morgan

Under the blue moon of this
whole silly business
really working for once, the people's poet
is reading to us from his most recent work.
Natty in tattersall,
boyish and fifty on the bare stage
under the blue light –
if the sidespots have rosecoloured filters, well
that won't wash with him –
listen,
his quick light voice not tripping ever
over his own peppery rhythms, the sibilants
and little silver sparks of spittle.
At first,
it was him blinking
into the black at the audience
and us wondering
had we backlit him too harshly,
bungled it again?
Imagine encouraging him to
leave his Antartex and his looseleaf
in the anteroom
and then him having to tiptoe
through all those ladies doing yoga
in helanca, stretching breaths,
just to rescue his poems!
He was nice about it,
nice about
the coffee we were sorry
not to be able to offer in the interval
and the low ticket sales.

Into his second poem
he seems in his element.
On the orange bucket-chair behind him

his wad of hardbacks and pamphlets.
That's all.The wall's
aerosol maze is ours,
the empty bottle,
painted guitar, and
at his feet somebody's rainbow scarf
a serpent
straight off a snakes-and-ladders board and
maybe it is a game
for him?
Certainly there is fun in it –
didn't the six
particle poems tickle us pink?
Then there was a witch, a cat, a broomstick
a sort of story for
Hallowe'en which it isn't,
though it was while he read it; there was
a mummy in need of urgent repair;
those transcripts of tapes from outer
outer space.
Yes. The woman pissing in Central Station
he wouldn't let us look away from
for one minute, our confusion, the celebration –
the celebration
(Callas, Nabokov, Bolan, Presley, Lowell)
of the loved lately dead. The Dance
that danced them off is not
what he ever praises (though
who can ignore it?)

Outside the buses throb and topdeck
passengers slide past at eyelevel, almost touchable,
Children shout clean into the cold.
The light from the public lavatory
catches the hurrying moon-
face of one girl and she's gone.
Taxis tick on
at possibly terrible cost.
But the winter city won't

stay locked shut
and that's what he sings out about.
It's chocablock with life
and lives we can make for.
(as next door
each yoga lady breathes
towards the new me)
Listen.
A Second Life.
Instructions to an Actor. –
it's mostly resurrection
he calls up in us.
There is no comfort in it.
Except the odd moment,
the ridiculous and the marvellous –
speaking with tongues to the hard of hearing
just for the hell of it
this poet is playing with pure sound
('there is no meaning in any ordinary sense.')
Listen,
the mad particles dance
stanza by stanza
the poem is becoming more miraculous
more clear.

Construction for a Site: Library on an Old Croquet Lawn, St Andrews

Nine Approaches

1.

Step down
into the silence, a green
pool.

2.

Forget
the sea is here.
From where you are
you cannot see
the sea.
Stop your ears.

3.

Swim
the length of this empty
pool, slowly.
Turn, anchor yourself dead centre.
Measure yourself one minute
against four green walls,
the domestic slant of the kitchen garden,
the perfectly right-
angled clipped box-hedge
and you're sunk.

4.

On the old croquet lawn
blackbird bounces
at his killing game.
On the site of the new library
accurate blackbird extracts

fat facts of worms.
Wink
back at him, he'll
zig off waggling
the tail-end of an idea.

5.

Listen,
chilly birdsong
sprinkling icewater
over the garden, a tap
turning on and off again.
Library silence.

6.

This is the lie of the land.
This is the house.
This is the staggered line of trees, Maytime
still struggling to bloom in a seawind,
daisies snatching shut-eye in the shade,
bluebells bruising blue, the late
late primroses on the cold slope.
This is the ironwork of the old gate.
It does not open.
It does not remind you of a prison.
This is the garden laid out for a gentle game
and when the garden grows
this is the wall that shelters.
This is the cut-out crowstepped arch
that frames the savage castle.
Don't
let history frame you
in a pretty lie.

7.

When
imaginary Alice in flimsy

muslin shivers slightly in
a heatwave in Nineteen Ten and
Hugh does a handstand on the barbered grass, hurrahs
as Frederick's mallet chips
a perfect one through oh refuse
to pretend to remember
the flavour of those
last of the raspberries that
Rab (cap-off) the gardener's
boy brought over (and which he did not taste).
Refuse to pretend to remember
how he and very decorated Frederick would both
be fattening worms in France
not six years later.
Freeze them in sepia.
Refuse to pretend to remember.

8.

the garden as mirror of man's logical scientific
   and ordered mind.
the library as garden.
the library as mirror of man's logical scientific
   and ordered mind.
the garden as game.
the game as mirror of man's logical scientific
   and ordered mind.
the game as mirror.
the mind as mirror of man's logical scientific
   and ordered garden.
the library as game.
Play the garden.

9.

The Formal Garden
(as the mind in the library) turns
in on itself. Croquet
and contemplation put us
through hoops. Consider.

Fourth of July Fireworks

The guests are gathered.
Boston-Irish Nancy, half in huff
says, 'Better help yourselves,
you all know Mister's timing well enough.'
Aside at me she mutters,
'Millionaires can afford to let things wait.
Honest-to-God Mister would be late
for his own funeral.' Cigarstore Indian,
I hide behind my apron, wait and drink in all I can.

(We don't exist. They pick our trays,
Tom Collinses, Martinis and canapés.)

Oh horror, New England night,
when I fetched the ice down and that snake
looped my feet in the kitchen garden! I still shake.
'Harmless,' says Nancy.
I hear her hiss, 'Some host!
That beggar'll only get here when he's sure he's last.'

Fourth of July. Cape Cod. Dead on cue,
last-man Mister comes running to his barbecue.
Arms flailing like a cricketer's across the lawn
from his 'so English' house with a flame red shirt on.

It's the cocktail hour. The air is still.
Mister gets busy on the charcoal grill.
Social-kissing women, backslapping men
has failed to break the ice. But then
Missiz appears like magic from the dusk.
Cool, ten years his junior, she smells of musk
and *Madame Rochas*. Two small spots of anger
high on her cheekbones linger.

When Mister says it's done enough
the guests spread ketchup on the fatted calf.

The night hots up. Liquor flows. Listless
couples come alive. A bit apart, restless,
Missiz sways gently on her own
to Glen Miller on the gramophone.
All eyes are on the soignee cling
of this year's leisure favourite, velvety stretch towelling
for patio-party wear. Those purples and electric pinks
'Just far too hectic altogether,' Nancy thinks.

(Ten years with Missiz, Nancy's face
is quite professional, impervious.)

Ice melts in the Martini tray. Midges
drown. The whole night edges
to a thunderstorm. Maybugs big as golfballs thud
as screendoors bounce them. But, after our blood,
divebombing mosquitoes dodge the mesh and slide
in down their own thin whine.
They bite despite insecticide.

All at sea,
white and dayglo orange fins spinnaker the bay.
Music blares
from the jazzed-up clubhouse round the Cape, Cotuit way
The whole damn town is two thirds empty after Labour Day
These summer people
migrate to Florida, lock, stock and barrel.
Tonight their parked cars sprawl the drive and trail
behind those his-and-hers coupled custom Cadillacs
like a comet trail.

(Oh I can see it all quite clearly, feeling small
and stone-cold sober. But I do not count at all.)

Out on the lawn the sprinklers, oddly luminous,
sputter like Roman Candles, ominous
as the sudden snap of queer clear light
from one weird streak unzips the dark.
The German Shepherd guard dogs bark.

A wind gets up. These beach-house boards
are flimsier than playing cards.

(Over the bay, like flares
odd rockets go up with a shock of stars.)

Mister drags off his box of fireworks to the shore.
Missiz drains her drink and hits the floor
with someone half her age. His snake-arms slur
around her waist. Eyes glaze. Sentence endings blur.
Missiz ('mutton dressed as lamb')
comes in slowly as the false-calm
lead-slow sea that slicks the beach. Sinatra sings.
The tide ravels up slowly, shelving things.

Raindrops big as bullets dent the roof we all stand under,
watching Canute's fireworks out-rage the storm,
try to steal its thunder.

The Carnival Horses

All along Hudson they are sanding down
the carnival horses.
Outside antique shops, so many, so
slender young men bend attentively
at the curlicued flanks, their
eyes and noses almost closed to dust,
the noxious effects of chemical paintstripper.
That mercenary bitch next door
brasso-ing the handles on a hope-chest
is nothing to them.
Like grooms with curry-combs
plying their wire-brushes
around the tossed head and
always wild eyes, whisking
the ears clean of paint-layers,
the gummed-up old notes of the hurdygurdy,
exposing the perfect quotemarks of the nostrils.
What is it
(*Falada*, *Falada*)
we wish that he would say?

Later when he's
skewered in a loft
somewhere in NoHo
silhouetted with his flung hooves and tassel-tail
re-gilded against prettily exposed brick
he'll make each
new owner who paid through the nose for him imagine
he feels the long slide down the sticky pole,
that he could ride again
the perfect carousel at the fair he never
ever went to
on his favourite chosen beast
he never even for a dime possessed.

Ontario October Going West

The wilderness tells the eye you won't
get very far with me says
tangle scribble says
pawmark and leafprint stippling layer on layer
says fernstitch herring-
bone   rusted wirewool to lie on   whisk-ear
blackthorn.
says strewn silky pillowstuffing   burst
milkweed.   says nudging
blunt bullrushes   (brown velvet)   fishhooked burr
bramble barb   vast feathery colourlessness.

The trees scream jaundice
canary   orange peel   adultery
oxblood   magenta.
the single drowned birch shrieks
fingerbone.
the lake says frankly this is
a very old trick   it's all
done with mirrors.

The barn (*see my
ancient white hex sign in a circle*) says
I'm twice as big and
beautiful as any house.
Winters like these   believe me
I have to be.

The railway says east west.

The prairie   when you get to it
says keep going.

Near Qu'Appelle

for Liz Allen

But then love she said
is almost always
surely she said
a strange country?
She had pale
seafarer's eyes that girl
there was ocean-glass
there were bits of seashell
on the windowledge
and outside the flat
colourless flat miles and miles
as far as what looked
very nearly blue but
was really only distance
and more of it.
You will recognise our house
she'd said.
It is the one up on –
jeez the prarie couple of
years here you learn to call
almost anything a hill.
First year more I thought
I would go mad the wind!
But then I'd married him
it was either that or go crazy.

She grinned and sunburn wind-
burn it did not matter which –
the long-ago
little-girl delicately hand-tinted
certainly still
recognisable photograph of her
in her own her other country
hanging behind her on the wall.

In Alberta

We have stopped by these
great big grain elevators marked with logo-wheat
stencilled Cargill   stamped Alberta Pool.
The boxcars
are just as clearly labelled
with destinations & capacities
numbers   warnings (*do not hump*
no climbing on roof).   Stopped
flat & nothing for it but for ten minutes
to examine the forged & intricate
ball & socket   ironwork   loop & pin   hand
fastened   engineered
male & female couplings between the cars &
exactly
how they work
how often break I honestly
don't know sweetheart.
In Alberta
there are oilwells like
loony mechanical chickens
dipping guzzling
& the man in the next seat says
in Alberta
everybody's applying for a divorce
says pair next door
common-law five years & then
the ceremony but she
goes off on this so-say holiday
in Salmon Arm   next thing
divorce.   He says no
it's not just the young ones
in Alberta
he says his brother
just damnwell
turned himself over in the dirt machine
lucky to be alive

lucky to survive.
Says he knew a man once
got squashed to nothing nobody
could recognise.
Says there's lots of big machines
could crush a man
in Alberta.

1. Sailing Past Liberty

for Rick Shaine

The first time I, well I think it was
that weekend, remember,
you'd gone to that
wedding in the Mid-
West, I was waiting it out with your
fat cat in Manhattan I must
have already decided my darling you
were worth waiting for ...

Early summer dust
on hot SoHo pavements, neon
scrawls New Wave on street cafés,
me walking holes in my five dollar
ropesole sandals – Little Italy
Chinatown, the Bowery, Wall
Street and Battery Park in a loud
bright bubble that was like assault
so the Staten Island Ferry seemed
the best of twentyfive cent bargains
(for tourism
was all I'd any reason then to think it was,
oh baby).
Then sailing past Liberty –
that string-quartet on the first deck
struck up for the fun of it, giving
us Vivaldi, and that fabulous skyline.
That great green
Harbour Lady, blank
containerships, gloomy hooters,
and one full-sail schooner.

Or maybe it was ...
anyway, months later,
twilight and very nearly winter
it felt out on that deck together

you saying it wasn't
what you gave up but what you gained,
the collar of your leather-
jacket up, you
sheltering me from the cold, no
we'd sailed
long past liberty by then,
those same bell-buoys rang eerily
that once rang in the new for
every immigrant who ever
entered Ellis Island hopefully.
(Dark eyes, I imagined
your grandfather in sepia
seeing this, holding tight
his little sister's hand.)

That was September, and
now I am here and
you are there
but that is neither here nor there
as far as what we feel
or what, together,
we will make happen.

And that white-card
cut-out of Liberty you sent her
graces my sister's Glasgow mantel-
piece, the week before her weddding.

2. Two Birds

on each of these two
cards from you blue-
tacked to the wall above
my writing table.
on

torn-edge Japanese hand-
made wood-paper flecked
with gold
two
bigwinged blacktipped wild
geese are caught in perfect
midflight assymetry on the blue
getting there.
and yet there's effort in it too,

the master artist does not deny it
– as on this cracked valentine
we found at the market stall, all
lovey-dovey these two
conventional circa
nineteen-ten bluebirds, one with
flower, one with billet-doux
above linked hands entwined
through hearts, a pretty
ditty about Constancy

that made us smile.
hearts are not
pretty frames for anything, all
rococo forgetmenots of cloying
Edwardiana.
they're raw and red
they jump, we know they do.

I say still: birds can be airmail blue
and hearts can be true.

3. My House

is now also your house
because you stayed in it too.

its walls have been printed
with your shadow.

coming home
there is still a faint
something of cigar
and a nickel that must have
fallen from your pocket.
and my bed
remembers your weight
as easily as my fingers do your hair.

Friday night and
the springs of the mattress
give an almost groan
not quite accepting me on my own.

4. Inter-City

Hammered like a bolt
diagonally through Scotland (my
small dark country) this
train's a
swaying caveful of half-
seas over oil-men (fuck
this fuck that fuck
everything) bound for Aberdeen and
North Sea Crude.
Empty beercans of
spun aluminium roll like ballbearings
underfoot and
sloshing amber's a
storm in whisky glass or two.
Outside's all
black absolutely
but for fizzing starbursts

of weirdblue or orange streetlights
and lit-up grids of windows.
Only bits of my own blurred
back-to-front face and
my mind elsewhere.
The artsyfartsy magazine I'm
not even pretending to read
wide open
at a photograph called Portrait of Absence.

5. In The Cutting Room

Working together (this
late) & below us with its
carchases
its sirens & sex
symbols the real
city flickers.
The Ramrod all-male cinema
and the twentyfive cent peepshow girls.

Here mister moviola you share
your high strange place
of stacked flat cans & numbered
glistening strips liked pegged
filmy stockings on a bathroom line
you are at work on them
in your small corner,
I in mine.
Chaste on Broadway, we moved
our privacy through the public streets.
The Brill elevator clanked us up through forty floors,
a water beetle big as a man's fist
scrabbling its corner.

You run it
over & over

forward back – one
dizzy whirr her scream shuts
& the woman in the white
night gown jerks herself backward
to the bed the nicely
glossed over
bad black sex.
Under the light of the
anglepoise I am
(beauty & the beast) at my business
of putting new twists
to old stories.

Working together & we seem
to love each other (but
that too is an old story)
yet not one of those fine few skills
(loops of language
spliced syllables of movement) we
have learned to curse but labour at
together   separate

No love is not a Steembeck
a heart is not
an editing machine – we can cut
out nothing   ignore everything
except what we want to see.
Ribbon of dreams,
have we put together too much
from scanty footage?

Ships

for John Oughton

We were
talking of ships, you
should have been there, you
would have seen them too.
Silent, slow, they slid their great bulks along the window
blocking half our light, coming
steaming in at tree-height
they anchored at the edge of everyone's vision.
This was not
ships that go bump in the night, absolutely
no boats bobbing in bathtubs but
big ships
with cargoes of portent.
Four poems, four ships, imagine.
My black sail:
the moon as a ghostly galleon:
Michael's 'wild ships of loon': and (for me)
it's mainly your imaginary icebreaker
I think of, ploughing
the white line up Hepbourne Street,
churning up the tarmac outside your house
and us adrift in your bed
wound in the sound of foghorns.

Once
for me to think of ships was to admit shipwreck,
maroon,
those utter inevitable deserted islands.
(The worst ships I saw,
did I ever tell you,
were those grey battleships in the half-light?
Menace, an unending
fleet of shapes glooming past
that balcony on the Bosphorus
all night the Night

Before the War Began.)
Don't think of them.

At every launching
there is held breath, wide eyes,
that glide
into a new watery world.
We don't need champagne to celebrate it.

Take this message.
It's oceanworthy,
it is a small ship in a bottle.
All night I have been tinkering with intricate riggings,
pulling threads,
to try and make it sail for you.

Hafiz on Danforth Avenue

There are no nightingales in this lunchroom, but
I have all these presents wrapped in that cheap
Christmas paper printed with those cardinals
you said sang out too loud.
Waiting for the
last of the breakfast specials I fish out
from the bottom of my handbag your father's
copy of Hafiz you lent me. Old ink
on the flyleaf, the name
that is also your name, the date
and where he bought it.

No place
for a lady here at eleven a.m.
in bitter mid December on the Danforth – all these
Greek men at the counter
on their rooted stools, sallow
under astrakhan, brindled moustaches,
the clack of worrybeads, I catch
a flash of amber and tassels.
A toothpick, a gold filling –
'Tonight I gonna finish one gallon of wine.
Tony makes it great. Forget
the mortgages, the pressure, tonight
if my wife she drives me I can get loaded.'

'A laughing winecup, a tangle
of knotted hair' I tingle
remembering us side by side – I am reading
your old Hafiz, you the New Divan I
brought with me, somehow linking
Glasgow to Toronto to Teheran.
Later you stretch out,
the book is closed on the carpet
a spiral of tangerine peel on the cover.

In the photograph you showed me Sunday
you are twelve, it is the year
you lived in Baghdad, you
are jug-eared, a proper cropped
North American boy.
There are two Iraqui taxidrivers,
a big Yankee car with
dangling charms of Islam. I can
smell the heat and the petrol.

'The morning breeze is the messenger of Love ...
The beloved
is sometimes the seller of sweetmeats,
the poet an eloquent sugarloving parrot.'
And today's snowflakes
muffle the mounds of Best Canadian
pumpkins and hubbardsquash outside
next door's greengrocery.
Here, through chromium and steam
the sugar dredger, a plate of lemons,
jellies, sherbert-coloured wedges
of chiffon pie.

The beautiful black waitress
wears a white beanie.

They've written Merry Christmas with glitterdust
on the mirror here in Motorama
beside the poster which says
Cold, Beautiful
Milk.
The young lovers
holding hands under the next table
play on the jukebox
'You don't bring me flowers.'

And to tell you this is easy,
scribbling this was as simple
as the shopping-list it jostles

on the next page of my notebook.
Love, as well as bread and coffee
it says eggplants, olive oil
don't forget
the nutmeg and cinnamon.

A Gift

When you come sometimes in what feels like secret
bringing a quick kiss
& a cargo of poems & photographs
(bringing in black & white
an armful of scratchy trees – those
typed soft words like desire & foghorn)
bringing yourself you bring me
the problem of acceptance.
What's this I say?
I've always been the one
giving
& guzzling & suffering with this love stuff.
I've been the one struggling at the words
I wanted written, not said.

So looking at your lines again
I melt & want to tell you I'm not jealous,
I know they're caused by loving.
& looking at your lines again (your body
stretched on my bed) the light
catching the surprising lines on your face
that show your age & I know are caused by laughing
I see
when well-meaning
other lovers brought you their gifthorses of nightmare &
selfhatred you somehow stayed unscathed.

Reading the Signs

never in my wildgoose dreams
before I came
(once there was the wildest
carchase only it was on
sort of skates in a strange changing
hill/cityscape & I
was winning not
that I had had to even find my feet on them
but they were brand new blades
& I
was sailing)
not even then did I imagine this
the ease of say
we're going somewhere by
favourite train
by car
there's music
or idle eavesdropping to be done
& anyway I can just sit
reading the signs
WINTERIZE NOW
MIDAS MUFFLER KING
loving the landscape looking
at you alternately not
much bothered which

& across the wide skies of Ontario
which are new but not strange are strung
the words of others
the notes of jazz are strung
lights and trees
these straggled vees of geese stay
threaded invisibly together like
Orion
or you & me

Flitting

Your place or mine, many a midnight
sees us shacked up somewhere and whose
bed is the better bet depends
whether we'd rather
tonight's permanent island
on a sea of chaos that's dis-
mantling itself or one
putting itself slowly together.

This summer I'm
splitting at the seams, I'm
full of it, my every
suitcase has its
teeth into this move. You've
spent a small fortune
on your big house.

It's either my Victorian reticules those
Biba fringes I'm going to throw out
dripping beads in the dark cramped round us,
or else your dead old lady's
velvet roses that
breathe the heavy weather and
'Miss Otis Regrets' outside your open window.

Either way
someone's used a strange toothbrush
and not sure it's wisdom
except we're at each other's throats all night
in blind tenderness
and in either
exact same other country we're dead easy.
You can make head and tail of me.

In the morning, a cause-
way to negotiate to whichever kitchen's

sketchy breakfast. You call me *sunshine*
which only goes to show
how little you know.

A Giveaway

I cancelled out the lines that most let on
I loved you. One week after I thought that it was done
and perfect, practically in print – here goes again
more of this that amateurs think of as tampering.
The tripe that's talked at times, honestly –
about truth and not altering a word,
being faithful to what you felt, whatever
that is, the *First Thought's Felicity*.
I have to laugh ... the truth!
You and me and no reason
for me to imagine I know the half of it.
I've said it time and time again,
listen, you've got to be ruthless,
if the rhythm's not right, it's not right,
it's simple
you've got to cut and cut and cut.
Rewrite.

Today's fair copy skips the scored out bit.
And all the better for it. That verse
set in the bedroom spoilt the form
and was never the issue anyway. Irrelevant.
At any rate I've gone to town on it all right
with black biro, blocked it out – hay
fever sneeze spill and kiss are all
the words even I can make out of it now.
Never could cancel with a single stroke!
Oh maybe it is a giveaway but don't
please be naive enough to think I'd mind
your knowing what I might invent of what I feel.
Poets don't bare their souls, they bare their skill.
God, all this
long apprenticeship and still
I can't handle it, can't
make anything much of it, that's my shame.
It's not an easy theme.

But finally I've scrubbed it, faced it, I know
the whole bloody stanza was wonky from the word go.

Heartbreak Hotel

Honeymooning alone
oh the food's
quite good (but it all needs salting).
Breadsticks admonish,
brittle fingers among formality – bishops' hats,
stiff skirts, white linen, silver implements.
This dining room
is all set for a funeral,
an anatomy lesson,
a celebration of communion
or a conjuring trick – maybe someone
will be sawn in half,
or a napkin could crumple
to an amazing dove.
Except
it's all empty
though I eat my helping
under a notice that says *This Place*
is Licensed for Singing and Dancing.

Go to your room.
What more lovely than to be alone
with a Teasmade, a radio and a telephone?
Loose end? Well, this is what you find
when you take the time off to unwind.
Empty twinbeds
and the space all hanging heavy
above your neat spare shoes
in your wall-to-wall wardrobe
underneath the jangling wires.

Honeymooning alone
can't get to sleep without the lights on,
can't swallow all that darkness on my own.
Syrup from the radio's
synthetically soothing late night show

oh remember, remember
then I reach to pop one of those press-stud pills
I keep under the pillow so
my system will stick tick next week
on the blink
a little crazily for you.
I can't sleep –
it's as livid as a scar
the white neon striplight
above my vanity bar.

Mirror, Mirror on the wall
does he love me enough,
does he love me at all?
Should I go back
with that celebrated shout?
Did my eyebrows offend you?
Well I've plucked them out.
Oh me and my mudpack,
I can't smile
my face will crack.
I'll come clean.
I've made good new resolutions
re my skincare routine.
Every day
there's a basket of blossomheads,
crumpled kleenex to throw away.
As if I found it easy to discard.
Think hard.
I've got a week to think it over
a shelf full of creams, sweet lotions
I can cover,
smother all my darkness in, smooth it over.
Oh it'll take more than this aerosol
to fix it all, to fix it all.

China Song

for Janice and John Gow, 1980

We are sitting pretty on our saucers.
Empty headed, not a thought
in our delicate trepanned porcelain
skulls, eggshell blue.
Admiring our own gold-bands, just like you
will be wearing in a day or two. And
when we say Wedding China
we want you to know we mean best bone
scarcely serviceable for every day.
And if you'd think
there'd be rather more
earthenware dished out these days
with so many marriages never winning
the tinfoil anniversary far less the wooden wedding,
still, we're glad to be wished-for, special,
nestled here in rustled tissue
beside the crystal you cannot see the future in.

Why I Gave you the Chinese Plate

for Kenny Storrie

I know how you feel
about ladies that dark and slim
and quiet and unlike me.
And chinoiserie.

I'm not sorry.
Neither are you what
I'd have thought I wanted.

In a landscape somewhere else
under a surface finely crazed with cracks
the silks of this painted girl instead
of all the dark girls you'll never have
as long as you keep wanting me to love.

Goldgreen, plum and jade
a nice glaze.
So choose
where you'll hang it
on the wall we might tear down.

Old Notebooks

Because she honestly
thought she'd like to learn to bake
good bread they
lugged the flour home
stone-ground from the flaxen mill.
Wanting to be whole
she pictured aprons sprigged with print
country kitchens
them sipping out of stoneware
a real couple
cutting, buttering another slice.

They tried to keep some always on the go –
yeast creaming itself in cups
something in a warm place rising
under a clean cloth (if they had one)
and but for the odd
leadballoon loaf it worked.
Telling themselves that
every batch got better
they cooked up good smells.
The tapped crust gave the proper
hollow sound.

Hard to remember
when they gave up the bran and went back
to bad habits grabbing
a quick sandwich at work and
forgetting to phone –
the apron all
balled up in the bottom of the laundry
for months with knotted strings.
So that now
opening old notebooks finding
recipes written in the hand

that was hers but no longer
slants quite the same she
does not sigh to think
they might have stripped the cupboard's pine
perhaps revealed a pleasing grain. Ah well
the half-hundredweight
sack of wholemeal slumped
like a corpse in the cubbyhole …
She shrugs, says
it soured we had to throw it out.

Fin

I know it's the end.
I can see it coming. I'm
like those women in the cinema who make you mad
fumbling for gloves
elbowing themselves into coats, buttoning up –
such a final snapping shut of handbags
the minute it looks like it's all over
but a change of mood and music.
So you demand response do you
right to the bitter end, you like
to see the credits roll?
I'm off.

That Summer

What you said before you upped and left
landed as splat as that
out-of-the-blue fat sheep at the
bottom of the cliff, the whole
heavy bellyful.
On my walk between the cottage
and the phonebox
I saw it disintegrate predictably
the pretty hooves
its only visible
bright eye dull and ooze
the usual moving
irridescence of bunched flies
on the matted pelt that was
nothing like the fireside sheepskin
we'd once been so smug about.
The whole sodden mess
gradually felted itself
flat and mashed into the long grass
among the cuckoo-slobber
and this was high summer.
The milled edge
of my tenpence piece
rasped at the slot
as I dialled the number of the flat
thinking of things growing fur
in the fridge, it ringing and ringing,
no one answering.

West Kensington

Wound-
up swaddled in your sleeping-bag in the living room
with stitched together thighs.
Shrugging it off
was shimmying out of a mermaid suit.
Thanks a bundle but
all the well-meant
extra blankets only
ended in a useless mound.
I've my own
manhandled luggage by me.
A sourish mouth from last night's Duty Free

Suddenly I can visit your bathroom and not question
whose eyebrow tweezers, why female shampoo.
You said to help myself and I did, but
had to watch I didn't wake you,
likely still well out of it two doors away,
what with the brassnecked kettle whistling
in the face of a brand new day.
I tiptoed with my toothbrush to the cold tap,
stirred bitter instant in a rinsed out cup,
snapped your sofa back
to a seated position.

And the funny thing was it didn't
seem funny.
I was fine
except your cats
came on to me all night.
Apart from that I slept all right.

As always. Any time,
any time, remember, I'd do
the same for you.

The Empty Song

Today saw the last of my Spanish shampoo.
Lasted an age now that sharing with you,
such a thing of the past is.
Giant Size. The brand
was always a compromise.
My new one's tailored exactly to my needs.
Nonspill. Protein-rich.
Feeds Body, promises to solve my problem hair.
Sweetheart, these days it's hard to care,
But oh oh insomniac moonlight
how unhoneyed is my middle of the night.
I could see you
far enough. Beyond me
how we'll get back together.
Campsites in Spain, moonlight,
heavy weather.

Today saw the end of my Spanish shampoo,
the end of my third month without you.

Noises in the Dark

The four a.m. call to the faithful wakes us,
its three-times off-key harmony of drones and wails.
Above our heads I snap the lightcord but the power fails
as usual leaving us in the dark. Tomorrow takes us
who knows where. What ruins? What towns? What smells?
Nothing shakes us.
We touch and today's too painful sunburn sticks and sears
apart again. Faithful to something three long years,
no fear, no final foreign dark quite breaks us.

Hotel habitues,
the ritually faithful wash their feet. Old plumbing grumbles.
The tap-leak in our rust-ringed basin tickles
irritant, incessant, an itch out of the dark. Whitewash crumbles
from the wall where the brittle cockroach trickles.
Fretful, faithful, wide to the dark, can we ever forget
this shabby town hotel, the shadow of the minaret?
Human or bird or animal? What was it cried?
The dark smear across the wall still unidentified.

A Letter

Your handwriting. A letterbomb
potentially. Blank side upmost on my mat
to turn it over was to trigger what
could blow my pieced-together calm.

In day thoughts a grey ghost.
livid in dreams. Damn you, I'm not blind
to the shock of your writing, its cockeyed slant, my mind
flips blank side uppermost.

What can you possibly want to say?
It fell so quietly I did not hear it drop.
White and flat and foreign, the envelope
does not give anything away.

Once letters flew like birds
between us. I'd read and read again, stuff
your spilling pages behind every clock and photograph.
They were full of everything but words.

This'll be the usual. The job's still fine,
I suppose? You'll ask me how are John and Di,
has Doreen had her baby, how am I
how's he and this new life of mine?

You talk of your new loves. Plural. Wild oats
at your age. Jesus, you should know better.
I'm mad at my own tears, but not enough to rip this letter.
Recently I've burnt nothing but my boats.

Though I confess that bitter confetti of the last one.
But that was in passion – these days it's far too late
for anything except to (eventually) reply to it –
the past that isn't dead enough to stuff a cushion.

Sundaysong

its about time
it came back again
if it was going to.
yes something's nesting
in the tentative creeper scribbling
Kellygreen felt tip
across our bedroom window.
hello.
its a lovely morning. we've got
full french roast for the enamelled yellow coffee pot.
there'll be transistors in the botanics
and blaring notes of blossom.
let's walk. let's talk.
let the weekend watch wind down.
let there be sun
let first you and me
and then breakfast and lunch be
rolled into one.

The Legend of the Sword & the Stone

I wish I wish we'd stopped before
It wasn't making love any more.

I had this trust. It broke.
Who was that lady ...? It's no joke.

But I dare you. Unzip my dress.
Turn me into an enchantress.

Enter with me on this act,
I will not give you back intact.

I am not flesh and blood and bone –
You are embedded deep in stone.

I know what witches know.
I won't free you, won't let you go.

Oh, but it was easy, withdrawing.
Smile on your lips, faraway look in your eye.
Oh how you whistled
as you knotted your necktie.
Wounding me
you left no scar
but bore away Excalibur.
New love. New War.

Rainbow

Listen you said
you never listen to a word I say
let alone the music.
This song you said
is beautiful. It's just about the finest thing
you ever heard. Listen to the cadences ...
that cord ...
Meanwhile the song rose and fell around us as
indifferent as rainfall
(it was pouring at the time) and all
that got through to me
was I heard you grow alternatively
labial and gutteral
as I watched your lips move
(and fell more and more in love)
and waited for a convenient lull
to put something a bit more in my line
on the record player.

Look I said
architect! You never use your eyes.
Colour I said
is just incredible. I'd go so far
as say it is the main thing. Well ... maybe
form is
for you purists. But see that colour sing,
the daffodils against that goldy thing,
those oranges in that pink plate.
What the *impressionists* ...
And in the clear light of that very moment
(the rain had just stopped)
the colour shimmered from the walls
and it buzzed, you couldn't pin it down.
Walls couldn't keep it flat or matt
on their simple surfaces.
It bounced from everything, it was

all around us.
And as I opened my mouth to say
So there and something about
form can't contain colour, you
kissed me on the nose
you laughed, you said
The way you look when you get het
up about something – oh
the colour you go!
Sweetheart you're vivid when you're livid.

Just then a convenient romantic rainbow
arched itself across our horizon.
It was a perfect one while it lasted –
it reached out for real roots
made for rainbow ends even.
Some colour! We couldn't
take our eyes off it for an instant
Hugged on the balcony
we were eavesdroppers on the whole hush.
And it hung there!

Then the gutters spilt liquid hilarity
from the full throats of their spigots like
a glockenspiel
We both heard it,
oh and we saw
odd drops from the windowledge make a
timpany of single notes,
each note shot with the spectrum.
Our rainbow arched and spread, grew
more and more vibrant until
it came to earth with a shock.

The Dollhouse Convention

Come to our one-day fair.
I suppose you could call it
almost a convention
of us miniaturists – the intricacy
of jewellers is absolutely
not wasted on us,
with base metals we can create
for instance this plaited replica
of an exact thumbnail breadloaf,
this tiny tray of taffy apples.
Aren't they sweet?

Loves, we must have such stuff to fill
our dollhouses with.
Bring your daughter, don't
bring her, we have stopped pretending
its only for the children we put on a show.
So if a setpiece says
Edwardian drawingroom scene,
whole family grouped round piano.
or *modern ranchhouse circa 1970 –*
note fatherfigure on a scaledown barcalounger
with minaturized playboy magazine –
remember we have sweated blood
worked with needles of astonishing thinness
in cloth and lace and realhair,
in paper and ceramic and spun glass
we tried to get the details right.
For what?
Is it for the mere satisfaction of seeing
into every room at once, even
the ones as children we were locked out of,
that we reduce
what we most deeply fear might be trivial
to what we can be sure
is perfectly cute?

In the Dreamschool

you are never the teacher.
The history lesson
goes on for ever.

Yammering the always
wrong answer to the hardest question
you stand up in nothing but
a washed-in vest.

In the dreamschool nothing can be covered up.
Fleeced, yellowing
you never learn.

Teacher is bigeyed behind
awesome bifocals
and his teeth are green.
An offered apple will only tempt the snake
curled under his chalkstripe jacket. Loch-
gelly, forked tongue, tawse.
Moonfaced mongols drag you towards
the terrible lavatories.

Sawdust soaks up sour mistakes.

2. The Teachers

they taught
that what you wrote in ink
carried more weight than what you wrote in pencil
and could not be rubbed out.
Punctuation was difficult. Wars
were bad but sometimes necessary
in the face of absolute evil as they knew only too well.

Miss Prentice wore her poppy the whole month of November.
Miss Mathieson hit the loud pedal
on the piano and made us sing
The Flowers of the Forest.
Miss Ferguson deplored the Chinese custom
of footbinding but extolled the ingenuity
of terracing the paddyfields.
Someone she'd once known had given her a kimono
  and a parasol.
Miss Prentice said the Empire had enlightened people
and been a two way thing.
The Dutch grew bulbs and were our allies in
wooden shoes.

We grew bulbs on the window sills
beside the frogspawn that quickened into wriggling
commas or stayed full stop.
Some people in our class were stupid, full stop.
The leather tawse was coiled around the sweetie tin
in her desk beside the box of coloured blackboard chalk
Miss Ferguson never used.

Miss Prentice wore utility smocks.
Miss Mathieson had a moustache.
If your four-needled knitting got no
further than the heel you couldn't turn
then she'd keep you at your helio sewing
till its wobbling cross-stitch was specked with rusty blood.

Spelling hard words was easy when you knew how.

3. The Prize

For Perfect Attendance was an easy one to win.
Bible stories for girls. Martha and Mary on the coloured
  frontispiece.

Your Sunday name in the Superintendent's copperplate.

It only meant being there, not 'paying attention'.
The Redemption hymnbook proved
the devil did not possess every best tune.

Red ticks like flyaway
flocks of birds sprigged the best exercise books.
Gold stars were favours given seldom as boiled sweets
in crinkled cellophane. X's were kisses
and kissing was wrong as all my sums.
Being first was top desk.
The doltish and dirty shared front row
with one sent down clever chatterbox in easy reach
of the teacher's ruler.

That September the squirrel
on the Shell country calendar wasn't on the wall
before Mattie won first death.
The weather chart said *Today it is Cloudy*
and my Top in General Knowledge
came of knowing the name for such a cloud
was Cumulus. We had to all turn over our jotters
and go over and over once again
till we knew by heart the Highway Code.

The Offering

Never in a month of them
would you go back.
Sunday,
the late smell of bacon
then the hard small feeling
of the offering in the mitten.
Remember how the hat-elastic cut.
Oh the boredom,
and how a lick of spittle got purple dye or pink
from the hymn-book you worried.
Maybe your neighbour would
have technicoloured pictures of
Jesus curing lepers
between the frail tissue pages of her bible
or she'd stroke you with the velvet
of a pressed rosepetal
till someone sucking peppermint
and smelling of mothball
poked you and hissed that you weren't to fidget.
Remember the singing
(with words and actions)
and how you never quite
understood the one about Nic-
odemus Coming to the Lord by Night.

Sunday,
perhaps an auntie
would visit with a cousin. Every Sunday
everyone would eat ice cream
and your mothers would compare you,
they'd stand you by the doorstop
and measure you up.

Sunday, maybe later in the evening
There'd be a Brethren Meeting.
Plain women wearing hats to cover

uncut hair. And
singing, under lamp-posts, out in our street!
And the leader
shouted the odds on Armageddon, he
tried to sell Salvation.
Everybody turned their televisions up.

Never in a month of them
should you go back.
Fond hope.
you'll still find you do not measure up.
The evangelist still mouths behind glass unheard.
You'll still not understand
the singing, the action or the word.
Ice cream will cloy, too sweet, too bland.
And the offering
still hard and knotted in your hand.

Legendary

I.

And if he was guilty
then it was of glibness.
He thought he could just whistle
but what he picked was too simple a song
(though an old one).
The North Knight found his lady fair –
toothsome smile
fifties glamour, tirling
a cheerleader's ponytail –
'The outlandish knight courted his lady fair
siller kaims for gowden hair'
and no he never noticed
the hammered-home nine mother-cursed combs of care.

Where had she come from?
He thought he saw it all.
The trick mantle seemed transparent enough.
He was dazzled.
Fishnet and what he took for spangles
but were fishscales (rapidly losing lustre)
from the day they dragged her
from the far Atlantic.
Certainly she fulfilled the conditions
coming neither clothed nor naked
neither riding or walking, and
carrying what was at once undoubtedly a gift
and yet nothing he should be grateful for.

Her wisecracks whipped him on.
It became a kind of contest.
When he set her impossible tasks
such as sew him a shirt without any seams or needlework
she laughed, sent home to mother for a copy
of Dressmaking Made Easy and McCalls' Pattern Book.

It was not
that she refused to recognise the magnitude of her problems,
just that for any real heroine
nothing is too menial –
at any rate in fairytales.
She knows inevitably she will come into her own.

So she turned his riddles inside out easily
like someone flyping pairs of socks
and threw them back at him.
Right at the start she told him
Death is colder than clay.
Poison greener than grass.
The Devil worse than any woman.
He just stood there
straddling the road
in all that clanging antiquated armour
turning brickred
coming slowly to his awful conclusion.
His blood sang out
She is Fit Mate.

II.

Easy for any outsider
to see they should have known better.
Even if it weren't for all the dipping they'd done
into all the legends which all went on at length
about this kind of catastrophe and carnage –
well, their own open eyes should have told them.
Bodies lay all around them
in the bonny broom, mutilated hideously.
And other versions of themselves
differently tinted
lay stiff and flat and parched
in photograph albums of former lovers.
The landscape was in an awful state.

But they went ahead with it.
They made the effort.

He was a deadeye marksman
but some of the silky things he brought home limp
she hadn't the stomach to make stew of.
When she scrambled the eggs he'd so carefully collected
purely to contemplate Creation Myths
he had to swallow it, say nothing.

She bought a Bendix. Had babies.
A pigeon pair.
Above all she wanted to be worthy.
he knew she confided to her diary
her honest malison and her good grudge
as she swelled monstrously, or was suckled at.
But she would sit there,
smoothing her gingham,
grimacing and knitting.
He knew she had it in her.
He wanted to shake her.

Soon he had to hunt further.
He had these three mouths that fed from him.
Sometimes he dreamed of them, sucking, accusing.
So often he left them all week
deep in the greenwood.

'What bluid's that on thy coat lap husband, husband?
Tell me the meaning of this stain I've found.

'Hawks' bluid was ne'er sae red, husband
lipstick that pink
whore's rouge that scarlet,
make my bed separate
make my bed soon
I'm weary wi living and fain wad lie doon.'

Next morning over plates of flakes
though too young to understand
the goshawk and the turtledow
spooning it in

could not but notice how
strange their parents had become.
Stiff figures. Playing cards.

And meeting her a month later
to discuss formalities, financial things,
the North Knight was struck by a commonplace pain.
My wife is a handsome woman
I can never love her again.

I have no idea what goes on inside her head.

One week later she was dead.

III.

And if a lily grew from her grave
round him he grew a briar.
And if a lily grew from her grave
and twined towards his breast
he would have none of it,
it was too like a mouthpiece
and its stalk
was too like a hotline down to her.
He tore at the roots of it.
He refused to talk.

And so he went on
living quietly
taking care of the children
buying them Clark's sandals
checking their fillings.

We do not know
whether in dreams
as in the legends
she comes as a birch

and with the jawbone of a salmon
and with the teeth of a pike

and her own yellow hair
a harp is made.

But if in the evening he should feel like a tune
and reach his fiddle down
it will never utter against him,
its strands are catgut
and the bow is not
a singing bone.
He is dry eyed,
says tears are not worth their salt.
And he owns
the voice he hears repeating, over and over,
I am guilty. Not guilty. Guilty. Not guilty.
It's not my fault.

Fetch on the First of January

Nae time eftir the Bells, and the
New Year new in wi' the
usual crowd, wi' whisky, cheers and kisses –
Ah'd aboot managed the windaes shut
some clown had thrown wide
hopin' tae hear the hooters on the Clyde
when the door went.
                                        Well, well,
who'd've though Ah'd be staunin' there
tae first foot masel'?

This some kinnuffa Huntigowk for Hogmany?
Hell-mend-ye, ye're
a bad penny, Jimmy –
Mister Ne'erdy Ne'er-do-Weel
sae chitterin' ill-clad for the caul'
sae drawn an' pale,
oh, wi' the black bun burnin' a hole
in yir poackit an' the coal
a Live Coal.

'Gawn, get' – Ah should shout it,
should shake a stick or ma fist,
oh but Ah should hunt ye, by Christ,
they wey you chased that big black tyke
that dogged ye wance, mind? –
a' the wey fae Hope Street hame.

Ah'll no let ye near me,
don't make me laugh,
got a much better
Better Half.
Och, aye tae glower at each other
was tae keek in a gey distortin' mirror,
yet ye've the neck to come back again
wi yir bare face, Jake Fetch,

the image o' my ain.
Ice roon yir mooth when ye kiss me
the cauld plumes o' yir breath
Ah'm lukkin' daggers
You're lukkin' like Death.
Ah'm damned if ye'll get past ma door,
nae fear!

Come away in, stranger, Happy New Year.

Mirror's Song

for Sally Potter

Smash me looking-glass glass
coffin, the one
that keeps your best black self on ice.
Smash me, she'll smash back –
without you she can't lift a finger.
Smash me she'll whirl out like Kali,
trashing the alligator mantrap handbags
with her righteous karate.
The ashcan for the stubbed lipsticks
and the lipsticked butts,
the wet lettuce of fivers!
She'll spill the Kleenex blossoms,
the tissues of lies, the matted
nests of hair from the brushes'
hedgehog spikes, she'll junk
the dead mice and the tampons
the twinkling single eyes
of winkled out diamante, the hatpins,
the whalebone and lycra,
the appleblossom and the underwires,
the chafing iron that kept them maiden,
the Valium and initialled hankies,
the lovepulps and the Librium,
the permanents and panstick and
Coty and Tangee Indelible,
Thalidomide and junk jewellery.

Smash me for your daughters and dead
mothers, for the widowed
spinsters of the first and every war
let her
rip up the appointment cards for the
terrible clinics,
the Greenham summonses, that date
they've handed us. Let her rip.

She'll crumple all the
tracts and the adverts, shred
all the wedding dresses, snap
all the spike-heel icicles
in the cave she will claw out of –
a woman giving birth to herself.

The Grimm Sisters (1981)

Illustration by Ingebjorg Smith.

The Storyteller Poems

I: Storyteller

she sat down
at the scoured table
in the swept kitchen
beside the dresser with its cracked delft.
And every last crumb of daylight was salted away.

No one could say the stories were useless
for as the tongue clacked
five or forty fingers stitched
corn was grated from the husk
patchwork was pieced
or the darning done.

Never the one to slander her shiftless.
Daily sloven or spotless no matter whether
dishwater or tasty was her soup.
To tell the stories was her work.
It was like spinning,
gathering thin air to the singlest strongest
thread. Night in
she'd have us waiting held
breath, for the ending we knew by heart.

And at first light
as the women stirred themselves to build the fire
as the peasant's feet felt for clogs
as thin grey washed over flat fields
the stories dissolved in the whorl of the ear
but they
hung themselves upside down
in the sleeping heads of the children
till they flew again
in the storyteller's night.

II: The Father

loving and bungling,
offending the evil fairy by forgetting
her invitation to the Christening,
or being tricked into bartering his beloved daughter
in exchange for the rose he only
took to please her –
then compoundig it all
by over-protectiveness and suppression
(banning
spinning wheels indeed
when the sensible thing would have been
to familiarise her from the cradle
and explain their power to hurt her).

But when she comes,
the beautiful daughter,
leading her lover by the sleeve, laughing –
'Come and meet my daddy, the King,
he's absolutely a hundred years behind the times
but such a dear.'
and she's (note Redeeming Kiss)
wide-eyed and aware.
Stirring, forgiven, full of love and terror,
her father hears her footstep on the stair.

III: The Mother

is always two faced
At best, she wished you
into being. Yes, it was she
cried at the seven drops of blood that fell,
staining the snow – she
who bargained crazily with Fate

for that longawaited child
as red as blood
as white as snow
and when you came true it was
she who clapped her hands merrily because
she was as happy as a Queen could be.
But she's always dying early,
so often it begins to look deliberate,
abandoning you,
leaving you to the terrible mercy
of the Worst Mother, the one who married your father.
She doesn't like you, she
prefers all your sisters, she
loves her sons.
She's jealous of mirrors.
She wants your heart in a casket.
When she cuts the apple in two and selflessly
takes the sour green half
she's good and glad to see you poisoned
by the sweet red pulp.
Tell me
what kind of prudent parent
would send a little child on a foolish errand in the forest
with a basket jammed with goodies
and wolf-bait? Don't trust her an inch.

The Grim Sisters

And for special things
(weddings, school-
concerts) the grown up girls next door
would do my hair.

Luxembourg announced Amami night.
I sat at peace passing bobbipins
from a marshmallow pink cosmetic purse
embossed with jazzmen,
girls with pony tails and a November
topaz lucky birthstone.
They doused my cow's-lick, rollered
and skewered tightly.
I expected that to be lovely
would be worth the hurt.

They read my Stars,
tied chiffon scarves to doorhandles, tried
to teach me tight dancesteps
you'd no guarantee
any partner you might find would ever be able to
keep up with as far as I could see.

There were always things to burn
before the men came in.

For each disaster
you were meant to know the handy hint.
Soap at a pinch
but better nailvarnish (clear) for ladders.
For kisscurls, spit.
Those days womanhood was quite a sticky thing
and that was what these grim sisters came to mean.

You'll know all about it soon enough.
But when the clock struck they

stood still, stopped dead.
And they were left there
out in the cold with the wrong skirtlength
and bouffant hair, dressed to kill,

who'd been
all the rage in fifty eight,
a swish of Persianelle
a slosh of perfume.
In those big black mantrap handbags
they snapped shut at any hint of *that*
were hedgehog hairbrushes
cottonwool mice and barbed combs to tease.
Their heels spiked bubblegum, dead leaves.

Wasp waist and cone breast, I see them yet.
I hope, I hope
there's been a change of more than silhouette.

The Furies

1: Harridan

Mad Meg on my mantelpiece,
Dulle Griet by Brueghel, a Flemish masterpiece
in anybody's eyes. 'Well worth historical consideration'
was how I looked at it. The surrealist tradition
from Bosch to Magritte is such a Flemish thing!
Oh a work of great power, most interesting ...
I chose it for my History of Art essay, took pains
to enumerate the monsters, reduce it all to picture planes.
I was scholarly, drew parallels
between Hieronymus Bosch's and Pieter Brueghel's Hells;
Compared and contrasted
Symbolism and Realism in the Flemish School;
discussed: Was Meg 'mad' or more the Shakespearean Fool?

The fool I was! Mad Meg, Sour-Tongued Margot,
maddened slut in this mass of misery, a Virago,
at her wit's end, running past Hell's Mouth, all reason gone,
she has one mailed glove, one battered breastplate on.
Oh that kitchen knife, that helmet, that silent shout,
I know Meg from the inside out.
All she owns in one arm, that lost look in her eyes.
These days I more than sympathise.

Oh I am wild-eyed, unkempt, hellbent, a harridan.
My sharp tongue will shrivel any man.
Should our paths cross
I'll embarrass you with public tears, accuse you with my loss.

II: Spinster

This is no way to go on.
Get wise. Accept. Be
a spinster of this parish.
My life's in shards.
I will keep fit in leotards.

Go vegetarian. Accept.
Support good causes.
Be frugal, circumspect.
Keep cats. Take tidy fits.
Go to evening classes.
Keep a nest-egg in the bank.
Try Yoga. Cut your losses.
Accept. Admit you're a bit of a crank –

Oh I may be a *bit* of a crank
but still I get by, frugally. Think positive.
I live and let live. Depend
on nobody. Accept.
Go in for self-improvement.
Keep up with trends.
I'll cultivate my conversation.
I'll cultivate my friends.
I'll grow a herbaceous border.
By hook by crook I'll get my house in order.

III: Bawd

I'll get all dolled up in my gladrags, stay
up till all hours, oh
up to no good.
It'll amaze you, the company I keep –
and I'll keep them at arm's length –
I've hauled my heart in off my sleeve.

I'll let my hair down,
go blonde, be a bombshell, be on the make,
I'll gold-dig, I'll be frankly fake.

I'll paint my face up, paint the town,
have carmine nails, oh
be fatal dame.
I've bold eyes, kohl sockets.
I'll look daggers, kill.
My lipstick colour's Merry Hell.

I'd frighten the French.
I'll be a torment, haunt men's dreams,
I'll wear my stockings black with seams.

I'll rouge my cleavage, flaunt myself, my heels
will be perilously high, oh
but I won't sway.
I'll shrug everything off the shoulder,
make wisecracks, be witty off the cuff.
Tell blue jokes in mixed company.

I'll be a bad lot.
I've a brass neck.
There is mayhem in my smile.
No one will guess it's not my style.

My Rival's House

is peopled with many surfaces.
Ormolu and gilt, slipper satin,
lush velvet couches,
cushions so stiff you can't sink in.
Tables polished clear enough to see distortions in.

We take our shoes off at her door,
shuffle stocking-soled, tiptoe – the parquet floor
is beautiful and its surface must
be protected. Dust
cover, drawn shade,
won't let the surface colour fade.

Silver sugar-tongs and silver salver,
my rival serves us tea.
She glosses over him and me.
I am all edges, a surface, a shell
and yet my rival thinks she means me well.
But what squirms beneath her surface I can tell.
Soon, my rival
capped tooth, polished nail
will fight, fight foul for her survival.
Deferential, daughterly, I sip
and thank her nicely for each bitter cup.

And I have much to thank her for.
This son she bore –
first blood to her –
never, never can escape scot free
the sour potluck of family.
And oh how close
this family that furnishes my rival's place.

Lady of the house.
Queen bee.
She is far more unconscious,

far more dangerous than me.
Listen, I was always my own worst enemy.
She has taken even this from me.

She dishes up her dreams for breakfast.
Dinner, and her salt tears pepper our soup.
She won't
give up.

Three Twists

I. Rapunzstiltskin

& just when our maiden had got
good & used to her isolation,
stopped daily expecting to be rescued,
had come to *almost* love her tower,
along comes This Prince
with absolutely
all the wrong answers.
Of course she had not been brought up to look for
originality or gingerbread
so at first she was quite undaunted
by his tendency to talk in strung-together cliché.
'Just hang on and we'll get you out of there'
he hollered like a fireman in some soap opera
when she confided her plight (the old
hag inside etc. & how trapped she was);
well, it was corny but
he did look sort of gorgeous
axe and all.
So there she was, humming & pulling
all the pins out of her chignon,
throwing him all the usual lifelines
till, soon, he was shimmying in & out
every other day as though
he owned the place, bringing her
the sex manuals & skeins of silk
from which she was meant, eventually,
to weave the means of her own escape.
'All very well & good,' she prompted,
'but when exactly?'
She gave him till
well past the bell on the timeclock.
She mouthed at him, hinted,
she was keener than a TV quizmaster

that he should get it right.
'I'll do everything in my power,' he intoned, *'but*
the impossible (she groaned) *might*
take a little longer.' He grinned.
She pulled her glasses off.
'All the better
to see you with my dear?' he hazarded.
She screamed, cut off her hair.
'Why, you're beautiful?' he guessed tentatively.
'No, No, No!' she
shrieked & stamped her foot so
hard it sank six cubits through the floorboards.
'I love you?' he came up with
as finally she tore herself in two.

II: Beauty & the

Beast
he was hot
he grew horns
he had you
screaming mammy daddy screaming blue
murder.
From one sleepy thought
of how like a mane his hair …
next thing
he's furred & feathered, pig bristled,
warted like a toad
puffed & jumping –
the green cling of those
froggy fingers
will make you shudder yet.
Then his flesh gone
dead. Scaled as a handbag.
He was that old crocodile
you had to kiss

yes, Rosebud, I
suppose you were right.
Better than hanging around
a hundred years for Someone
to hack his way through the thorns
for the shoe that fits
for chance to have you cough up
the poisoned apple
wodged in your gullet.
So you (anything for a quiet
life) embrace the beast, endure.

Three days & nights, three patient years,
you'll win I'm sure.
But who'd have guessed
paying your dues would mean
the whole wham bam menagerie?

Oh, but soon
(her hair grew lang her breath grew strang)
you'll
(little One-Eye for little Three-Eyes, the
Bearded Lady)
Yes, sweet Beauty, you'll
match him
horror for horror.

III: After Leaving the Castle

On the first night
the lady lay in the dark with her lover
awake all night
afraid her husband would pursue her.

On the second night
the lady lay awake in the arms of her lover

her tongue and teeth idly
exploring the cold of his earring.

On the third night
the lady lay awake afraid
her husband would never come after.

On the fourth night
the lady thought as she drifted off to sleep
how monotonous it was going to be
to live on rabbit stew forever
& she turned a little away
from snoring, the smell of wild garlic.

When they passed him on the road
on the fifth day,
she began to make eyes at the merchant.

Tam Lin's Lady

'Oh I forbid you maidens a'
who wear gowd in your hair –
to come or go by Carterhaugh
for young Tam Lin is there.'

So you met him in a magic place?
OK
But that's a bit airy fairy for me.
I go for the specific – you could, for instance,
say that when he took you for a coffee
before he stuck you on the last bus
there was one of those horrible congealed-on
plastic tomatoes on the table ... oh don't
ask me
I don't know why everything has to be so sordid these days ...
I can take *some* sentiment –
tell me how charmed you were
when he wrote both your names and a heart in spilt coffee –
anything except that he carved them on the eldern tree.
But have it your own way.
Picking apart your personal
dream landscape of court and castle and greenwood
isn't really up to me.
So call it magical. A fair country.
Anyway you were warned.

And if, as the story goes nine times out of ten –
he took you by the milkwhite hand & by the grassgreen sleeve
& laid you on the bonnie bank & asked of you no leave,
well, so what?
You're not the first to fall for it,
good green girdle and all –
with your schooltie rolled up in your pocket
trying to look eighteen. I know.
All perfectly forgiveable.
Relax.

What I do think was a little dumb
if you don't mind me saying so
was to swallow that old one about you being
the only one who could save him.

Oh I see – there was this lady
he couldn't get free of.
Seven years and more he said he'd sacrificed himself
and if you didn't help him he'd end up
a fairy for ever! Enslaved.

Or worse still in hell without you.

Well, well.
So he stopped you from wandering in the forest
and picking pennyroyal and foxgloves
and making appointments and borrowing money for the
abortion.
He said all would be well
If only you'd trust him just this once
and go through
what he was honest enough to admit in advance
would be hell and highwater for you.

So he told you which relatives to pander to
and which to ignore.
How to snatch him from the Old One
and hold on through thick and thin
through every change that happened.
Oh but it was terrible!
It seemed earlier, you see,
he'd been talking in symbols (like
adder-snake, wild savage bear
brand of bright iron red-hot from the fire)
and as usual the plain unmythical truth was worse.
At any rate you were good and brave, you did
hang on, hang on tight.
And in the end of course
everything turned out conventionally right

with the old witch banished to her corner lamenting,
cursing his soft heart and the fact she couldn't keep him,
and everyone sending out for booze for the wedding.

So we're all supposed to be happy?
But how about you, my fallen fair maiden
now the drama's over, tell me
how goes the glamourie?
After the twelve casks of good claret wine
and the twelve and twelve of muskadine,
tell me
what about you?
How do you think Tam Lin will take
all the changes you go through?

Six Disenchantments

The mirror you are
tells me too often
I am not beautiful.

The warm room you were once
was a good place to be.
Oh catch me saying
the walls of the room were warm fingers stroking
but it was clean and decent,
it was the kind of place that let me warm myself.
I spent a lot of time in it
scribbling and humming, rearranging
at my leisure
the objects on the mantelshelf.

The rocket you are
still takes off occasionally
with a bump and a woosh in the night.
Always, it's always the surprise of my life
and I have to hang on tight.

You say the scissors I am
are too keen on cutting.

You say the teacher I am
is a terrible version of a cartoon schoolmarm
too straightlipped and square shouldered
all pinstripes and pencil skirt, spike heels, she's
strictly
too lewd to be true
and you can't be sure what punishment
she wants to exact from you.
So you thumb your nose and tell her
her boys will all grow up too soon
leave school and throw their schoolcaps
over the moon.

God
the brickwall you are these days
it doesn't even crack when you smile.
Believe me I spent a lot of time
working with my fingernails at mortar and lime
before I started to bash and
batter my head at it, that brick wall.
Now, even when I stop,
it doesn't stop hurting at all.

Part Two: The Beltane Bride

The Beltane Bride

Yestreen the queen was wyce enough
To forswear all desire
From limerance and venery
She flinched as at fire.

She said she'd love to live with him
But she was not that kind
She'd raither lie in ironed silk
And in her right mind.

He pu'd the dress from her shooders
And a' the pins from her hair
And he easily undid her tidy life
But the ladye didna care …

'Tho' shairly I'm fond
Tho' they a' ca' me fool
I'll lie under this crazy quilt
wi' my Lord of Misrule.'

Song Of Solomon

You
smell nice he said
what is it?
Honey? He nuzzled a soap-trace
in the hollow of her collarbone.
The herbs of her hair?
Salt? He licked
a riverbed between her breasts.

(He'd seemed
not unconvinced by the chemical
attar of roses at her armpit. She tried
to relax have absolute faith in
the expensive secretions of teased civet to
trust the musk at her pulse spots
never think of the whiff of
sourmilk from her navel
the curds of cheese between the toes
the dried blood smell of many small wounds
the stink of fish at her crotch.)

No there he was above her apparently
as happy as a hog rooting for truffles.
She caressed him behind the ear
with the garlic of her cooking-thumb.
She banged shut her eyes
and hoped he would not smell her fear.

Stooge Song

How did I get here?
Out of my
streetclothes & into
these sad spangles
having the silken flags of many countries
dragged from between my ears,
the perfect egg
coaxed from my cleavage,
it's undignified.
How did I get here?
The children chorus YOU VOLUNTEERED

& oh yes I
do
seem to remember myself
long ago
safe in the dark on the other side of the orchestra pit
laughing & munching
on those sweets I'd caught, that Buttons threw …
then I sort of recall
something about him leaning over the footlights
& me telegraphing furiously
CHOOSE ME CHOOSE ME

& it isn't as if I ever
liked him did I? Surely
I can't have been taken in
by his blackpatent hair & his permanent grin?

Shall I let you into a little secret?
Let me tell you what's what.
Can you keep it under your hat?

There is No Easter Bunny.
There.
Pure illusion & so are

(big gimmick)
those hawks he teases out of handkerchieves
instead of doves.
It wasn't Real Claws
that made such short work
of my
long
kid gloves.

Right on cue he
takes my hand &
I stammer out
that bit about
I HAVE NEVER SEEN YOU BEFORE YOU IN MY LIFE
but I must have my lines all wrong again,
all the people laugh.
& NOW, THE GRAND FINALE
THE LITTLE LADY WILL BE SAWN IN HALF

& oh (here we go again) truly
I have
never had my head so
effectively separated from my body
Look I can wiggle my toes, can
wave tinkly fingers from
the four corners of the stage.
I volunteered. It was
all my own idea to come up here.
I smile & smile & smile to show my rage.

Midsummer Night

Was that a donkey braying in my dream?
Couldn't make head or tail of it but
it hawhawed itself blue in the face
whatever it was. Still, Confusion's clearly
what's called for in any comedy worth worrying about.
That and Chance
which certainly seems to be
playing its part all right.
So we're laughing?
Get us, half enchanted and undecided
whether or not to give in to it,
wandering the wide woods on such a night like
the wrong pair of ill-met demi-
lovers we most likely are
in far too high a pollen count for
anybody's comfort. This is the
silly season though – you said so yourself –
surely a solstice is a time for going to extremes.
Have a heart though, I've always been
the equinox sort – white nights
and talking till birdsong
are as new a taste to me as the
piney retsina we sat late in the restaurant with,
till one. And still no real dark yet
to go home in.

Earlier, between
the World Cup and Wimbledon the blue
TV lights flickered from every douce house
in the solid suburbs we drove through to come
to such a shifting place.
Remember the horses
how silently they moved
from dark woods.
'Would you call this a green glade?' you
asking gravely with a glint,

the lilac haze and three rooks on the long meadow,
that russet shape that changed
we could swear it, and stretched
and lengthened to a fox and back to prick-eared
hare again. Nothing tonight could decide
what form to take.

We are good and strange to one another and no mistake.

Blueshirt

Halfway
into your blue
and white striped shirt you stop
and gather me up once more
against your dark
before you button yourself into the day.

Well break-
fasted I move
alone and trusted
among your books and jazz
your photographs (horn-
players friends and trees)
I scribble at your table hang
my three clean shirts
in your closet am caught
in the cold cold stare of the tiger cat
I know was named by the lady
you say left long ago.
There's no snapshot of her taped up
not so much
as a hairpin in the bathroom cabinet.

An hour ago
you whistled off to work
leaving a kiss a spare key
and no conditions.
Like Bluebeard's wife
I stare at this key printed on my palm
its intricate notchings
then (absolutely clean
of charms or chicken bones) I
pocket it.
In your innocent ticking fridge
I might find the forbidden egg
crowned with blood.

The Hickie

I mouth
sorry in the mirror when I see
the mark I must have made just now
loving you.
Easy to say it's alright
adultery
like blasphemy is for believers but
even in our
situation simple etiquette says
love should leave us both unmarked.
You are on loan to me like a library book
and we both know it.
Fine if you love both of us
but neither of us must too much show it.

In my misted mirror
you trace two toothprints
on the skin of your shoulder and sure
you're almost quick enough
to smile out bright and clear for me
as if it was OK.

Friends again, together in this bathroom
we finish washing love away.

The Other Woman

The other woman
lies
between us like a bolster.
When I hit out wild she's
insubstantial, a
flurry of feathers, a mere
sneezing irritant.
When my shaped and hardened words turn
machine-gun
against you she's rock solid
the sandbag you hide behind.

The other woman
lies
when she says she does not want
your guts for her garterbelt.
I send out spies, they say relax
she's a hag she's just a kid
she's not a patch she's nothing to she's
no oil painting.
I'd know her anywhere.
I look for her in department stores, I scan
every cinema-queue.
Sometimes suddenly in some downtown restaurant
I catch her eye
casting crazily around for me.

The other woman
lies
the other side of my very own mirror.
Sweet, when I smile
straight out for you, she
puts a little twist on it, my
right hand never knows what her left is doing.
She's sinister.
She does not mean you well.

Last Supper

She is getting good and ready to renounce
his sweet flesh.
Not just for lent. (For
Ever)
But meanwhile she is assembling the ingredients
for their last treat, the proper
feast (after all
didn't they always
eat together
rather more than rather well?)
So here she is tearing foliage, scrambling
the salad, maybe lighting candles even, anyway
stepping back to admire the effect of
the table she's made (and oh yes now
will have to lie on) the silverware,
the nicely al-
dente vegetables, the cooked goose.
He could be depended on to bring the bottle
plus betrayal with a kiss.

Already she was imagining it done with, this feast, and
exactly
what kind of leftover hash she'd make of it
among friends, when it was just
The Girls, when those three met again.
What very good soup
she could render from the bones,
then something substantial, something extra
tasty if not elegant.

Yes, there they'd be, cackling around the cauldron,
spitting out the gristlier bits
of his giblets;
gnawing on the knucklebone of some
intricate irony;
getting grave and dainty at the

petit-gout mouthfuls of reported speech;
'That's rich!' they'd splutter,
munching the lies, fat and sizzling as sausages.
Then they'd sink back
gorged on truth
and their own savage integrity,
sleek on it all, preening
like corbies, their bright eyes blinking
satisfied
till somebody would get hungry
and go hunting again.

Part Three: Hags and Maidens

Everybody's Mother

Of course everybody's mother always and
so on ...

Always never
loved you enough
or too smothering much.

Of course you were the Only One, your
mother
a machine
that shat out siblings, listen

everybody's mother
was the original Frigid-
aire Icequeen clunking out
the hardstuff in nuggets, mirror-
silvers and ice-splinters that'd stick
in your heart.

Absolutely everyone's mother
was artistic when she was young.

Everyone's mother
was a perfumed presence with pearls, remote
white shoulders when she
bent over in her ball dress
to kiss you in your crib.

Everybody's mother slept with the butcher
for sausages to stuff you with.

Everyone's mother
mythologised herself. You got mixed up
between dragon's teeth and blackmarket stockings.

Naturally
she failed to give you
Positive Feelings
about your own sorry
sprouting body (it was a bloody shame)

but she did
sit up all night sewing sequins
on your carnival costume

so you would have a good time

and she spat
on the corner of her hanky and scraped
at your mouth with sour lace till you squirmed

so you would look smart

And where
was your father all this time?
Away
at the war, or
in his office, or any-
way conspicuous for his
Absence, so

what if your mother did
float around above you
big as a barrage balloon
blocking out the light?

Nobody's mother can't not never do nothing right.

The Ariadne Version

Of course Ariadne was in it
right up to here,
the family labyrinth – lush
palatial and stained with sacrifice.
Maybe money grew on trees
for Minos in summer Crete but
Ariadne, imagine it,
sizzling on the beach all day
with school out
or mooning around in that room of hers
tricked out chintzily
to her mother's fond idea of some subteen dream –
all those Daedalus dolls dangling, for godsake.
Someone should realise at Ariadne's age
they were just not
amusing any more.
Oh they gave her arty crafty kits
for her birthday – balls
of silver filigree fingering
to keep her hands busy at any rate with
tatting or
crochet or some such crap.
No one would admit it.
It had burst inside her recently
like a bull in a china shop.
She was grown up.
She had to get the hell out, somehow.
But talking to them was
bashing your head against a brick wall,
when it came to unravelling anything
they just weren't interested.

Big Daddy would just do his Kingpin bit,
lay down the law.
And her moonstreaked mother had gone blonde again,
mincing around in that rawhide trouser suit,

all silicone and facelift – must be off again
after some big bronzed stud in the palace guard.
Her father was turning a blind eye as usual –
if he'd objected everytime she made him wear the horns
she'd only have dredged the past again
and hurled at him every nymph he'd ever
given the palmgrove treatment.
Ariadne lay wide awake listening
to the quarrelling leak through leadlined walls.
Worse was the love.
Some labyrinth. It fitted them like a glove.

Ariadne lay on the silver sands
applying more Ambre solaire
(she was browning nicely).
Ariadne decided
she'd be off like a shot with the first man
who looked halfways likely,
so she'd better
kill off her own brute bit
her best friend, her brother,
doll-up to the nines go ultra
feminine (one hundred percent).
The sea roared and pounded.
Over the far horizon
appeared a black sail …

Poem for my Sister

My little sister likes to try my shoes,
to strut in them,
admire her spindle-thin twelve-year-old legs
in this season's styles.
She says they fit her perfectly,
but wobbles
on their high heels, they're
hard to balance.

I like to watch my little sister
playing hopscotch, admire the neat hops-and-skips of her,
their quick peck,
never-missing their mark, not
over-stepping the line.
She is competent at peever.

I try to warn my little sister
about unsuitable shoes,
point out my own distorted feet, the callouses,
odd patches of hard skin.
I should not like to see her
in my shoes.
I wish she could stay
sure footed,
                sensibly shod.

My Mother's Suitors

have come to court me
have come to call oh
yes with their wonderful world
war two moustaches their long
stem roses their cultivated
accents (they're English aren't they
at very least they're
educated-Scots).
They are absolutely
au fait with menu-French
they know the language of flowers
& oh they'd die
rather than send a dozen yellow
they always get them right & red.
Their handwriting on the florist's card
slants neither too much to the left or right.

They are good sorts.
They have the profile for it – note
the not too much nose
the plenty chin. The
stockings they bring have no strings
& their square
capable hands are forever
lifting your hair and gently
pushing your head away from them
to fumble endearingly at your nape
with the clasp of the pretty heirloom
little necklace they know their
grandmother would have wanted
you to have.
(never opals – they know
that pearls mean tears).

They have come to call & we'll all
go walking under the black sky's

droning big bombers
among the ratatat of ack-ack.
We'll go dancing & tonight
shall I wear the lilac, or the
scarlet, or the white?

Girl's Song

My father
would warn of the danger. Eggs all
in one basket. Pride hurtling for its fall.
One swallow does not make a summer,
he'd have me remember.

I'm seven, I'm
over the moon.
I've a brand new coat of bright red stuff.
My father asks me is it warm enough.

I'm twenty four, I
go over the score.
In my father's eyes I'm all but lost.
I want magenta and pentecost.

This letter
is from my father. He forwards mail and
drops a quick line in his careful hand.

How am I for money? Am I sure I've enough?
Farther forgive. Though it's hard to read
you sign *with love*.

The Cailleach

Bitter Winter
won't let up
never stop
the old stranglehold.

Bluemoon
crystalgazer's
done her stint of wintering.
Highhanded
hardbitten
her rigour
will outlast
austere
dogstar's
deathwatch stringencies.

Brittle sun
spiking light's just
grist
to Winter's mill.
She's all set to put us through it.

She'll crack down
old Mama Iron Heel
she'll make us rue it.

Poppies

My father said she'd be fined
at best, jailed maybe, the lady
whose high heels shattered the silence.
I sat on his knee, we were listening
to the silence on the radio.
My mother tutted, oh that it was terrible,
as over our air
those sharp heeltaps struck steel, rang clear
as a burst of gunfire or a laugh
through those wired-up silent streets around the Cenotaph.
Respect.
Remembrance.
Surely when all was said
two minutes' silence in November
wasn't much to ask for, for the dead?
Poppies on the mantelpiece, the photograph
of a boy in a forage cap, the polished
walnut veneer of the wireless,
the buzzing in the ears and when
the silence ended the heldfire voice
of the commentator, who was shocked,
naturally, but not
wanting to make too much of it.
Why did she do it?
Was she taken sick – but that was no
excuse, on the radio it said,
couldn't you picture it?
how grown soldiers buttoned in their uniforms
keeled over, fell like flies
trying to keep up the silence.
Maybe it was looking at the khaki button eye
and the woundwire stem
of the redrag poppy
pinned in her proper lapel

that made the lady stick a bloody bunch of them
behind her ear
and clash those high heels across the square,
a dancer.

The Last Hag

The last hag
I have her
nailed. Corndolly, a hank of straw, old
spindleshanks
dried up. A relic.
The last word in the folksy bit
bunched in her dirndl with sticky
burrs with poppypods'
deathrattle.
I've cut her down to size at last,
old hasbeen
always at me with
her witchy whispering
saying daughter, successor –
so much salestalk
for all that growing stuff.
I stopped my ears.
I strung her up above my high wide bed.
She'll shrivel, I'll sleep
solo curled and small but sound. Seems right.
Could be good
to go underground a while.

I want to winter a bit,
honestly.
Take pleasure as I move
in empty rooms
arrange dry grasses.
Sweet to see my own stored pulses
shelved.
Bottling plenty – oh you'd not believe
the goodies I've got
salted away.

Take each day
one in front of the other.
hayfoot strawfoot that's how.

And in my own good time
I'll let rip again.

Islands
(1978)

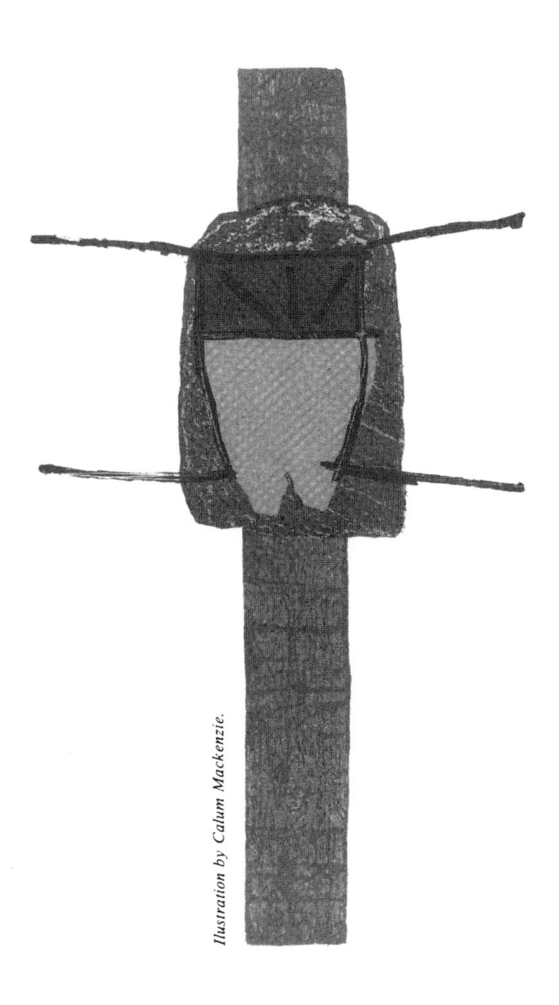

Illustration by Calum Mackenzie.

Outer

I

Another life
we marvel at the tweeds
a bale by each gatepost.
This is the day the lorry will collect
granite-marl   green-lovatt
herringbone   houndstooth   rust and
heathermix.

From each dour house
always this always black
and white dog comes to stand stock still.
He's only ruffled by the wind.
He doesn't waste a bark. He's only
here to check we skirt his land.

Another life
each spare rib croft
each staggered drystane wall
that makes slicing up bare land
look next to natural.
Low houses   separate   strung across the hill
so far away from us –
the woman on the doorstep with a basin
that might be henmash
or monday washing
the man
shut in with the bare bulb
and the clattering in the blacktarred hut
where the weaving gets done.

Lambs home in
Two hard tugs
and they fasten onto each vague mother.
Absentmindedly it seems

sheep tug at the roots of everything
till it's all baldness, stones and droppings.
Hens scratch and pick.
The flagrant cockerel's let crow
from the boss-eyed skull of a rusted truck.
Bones, blackhouses, implements,

things fall to bits.
Sheep come apart in handfuls –
it's that time of year –
old cars in the salt air,
Far too many stones to ever clear.

What's not useful lies and rots.
Useless to say *ramshackle*
or to call it waste.
Nothing goes and leaves no trace –
just that here's a climate where
it's all meshed over, nettled, part of things
in no time. Absorbable.
Rain and mud and wind
will streak and fritter even this too-blue
plastic feedbag till it blends.

Even the weaving will go to the wall
(the hand-
loom's finished if this doublewidth comes in)
Shawbost, Breger, Arnol who'll
make ends meet?

For there's a bare living only
if even the godless can pass Sunday
decently idle in their stocking soles
and never cross the door.
If you use the otterboard to trick the fish
and without your nosey neighbour knowing
fit a motor that will turn your loom.
If you don't get caught.
If you can keep the sheep out

your patch might learn a smattering of growth.
Wind combs out wool wraithed
on nebulous, necessary fences.

II

And so we go to Callanish to see the stones.
Another world entirely.
Chill at the bone
we walk the longest limb avenue of stones all
twice as tall as any man.
Nowhere on this island can you find this stone.
Who brought?
Hard and how far? Why?
Purpose a plain use our bones root to remember.
long-before Christ   precisely cruciform   a calendar
a seasons-map   magical
and more.
Human bones at the crux. A skull. A chamber
inside the certain circle of these standing stones.
Long before the solstice we'll be gone.
We won't see the silver giant
rise and walk at dawn.

III

And when the butter wouldn't churn
there was a saying if you took a pan –
having first shut fast the windows and the door –
and gave some of that slow milk
a right good scald over the fire
the witch that was the one that cursed it
had to come.
It worked.
The auld bitch knocked my father said
and afterwards the village knew her.
Over our drink it seems
Dolidh will tell us – if she's pressed –
of the witches of Tolsta.

And och it's all nonsense
but then his mother's sister was supposed
when she was only young
to have been half-promised
before she thought the better of it to this lad.
Who could understand it?
It was she who did the jilting
but she lost every bit of colour
and every day she grew more thin.
Her mother sent her to the White Magic Man
six miles away. Herbs
and a prayer. He said walk back
but remember not to speak
before you cross your own doorstep.
And on the way
she met that lad's mother and was forced
to return her good-day.
She wasted. Still she got thin.
until her mother sent her to the Man again.
He said
I told you not to talk.
Go back.
Once more as she was walking she met the lad's mother
This time she didn't answer.
She got better.
Later it was said
someone found a clay doll under running water.

Donald gives us more malt
Dolina pokes the fire.
Midsummer but we shiver
thinking of the slow wearing away of water.
She draws us closer in.

IV

wind hurts
old molar
hollow stump blunt tooth bare

round and round
this broch
will baffle still

stonewall
doublebluff
drystane

harshness of that winter
watched
and when the cry went up
walled in between
the dark invader
and the women young and beasts
between stone walls
was chance of surviving for these men.

dun carloway we
crawl the long ramp
between the inner and the outer
wall again.

V

Golden Harvest.
The Girl Pat.
Eilan Glas.
Naturally sixteen has not much time
for all the old songs.
These two have dogged the Mod
this last afternoon, undone
the top three buttons, folded
shirt-collars open to a deep vee –
schoolgirls arm in arm
down by the harbour humming.
Arm in arm
on such high cork shoes they still
move easily

among oil and rope and smeared
rainbows of fishscales.

They giggle
or go blank
or bat back smart answers
to the young dogs (sealegs,
cuffed wellingtons) moving easily
among nets and hooks and weights.
Luminous floats,
wolf whistles.

Trouble is this town's too small.
They've twice trawled around the circuit
of mainstreet and back round church street,
sneered at every white-net Sunday hat with streamers
in the Pakistani draper's shop display.
In the autumn there's the nursing.

At Woolworth's beauty counter
one smears across the back of her hand
the colour of her next kiss.
The other nets in her wiremesh basket
Sea Witch.
Harvest Gold.

VI

Laura has gone in a clean white blouse
to Stornoway to sing Beginners Gaelic in the Mod.
Eeshy and Agnes-Mhairi
always laugh she says
and imitate the way incomers talk.
Let them she says.
living here she wants to learn.
Eleven-years-old,
she'd rather be here than Glasgow anyday.
This is where she wants to stay.

She opens her book. She shines.
We stumble after her, repeat.

Is e seo tigh ban.
Is e seo tigh dubh.
This is a white house.
This is a black house.

Inner

I

make a change
if you get the weather

yes the place we're staying in
is green

bracken comes out clenched
only unbends
in the company of many others.
rigid, sinister as soldiers,
won't let us pass.

need not-English –
don't want to know the silly pretty names
for wildflowers
when I look them up in Sarah's book.
starlike in wiry grass
Skye flowers are too wild to call
Seapink Kingcup Lady's Smock.
another language.
last week on Lewis
Jim said he'd found that Gaelic words for colours
weren't colours as he thought he knew them.
chrome-yellow red-spectrum unsayable
straight from the tube.
rather a word might mean
red or reddish-brown earthbound.
another black or deep or purplish –
the colour of the darkness.
blue a clearness.
takes time says Jim
to know exactly how to paint here.
such distinctions.
glàs

might mean green or even calm-sea grey.
more a chroma of the weather
colour of the mind.

II

the birds
at first they bothered me
so big
so strange
their cries

just who
is that cuckoo
getting at all day?
the mechanical lark
on its yoyo string
the crossbow shadow of the hawk.

only took
two hooligan gulls
to chase that eagle round in circles
for half an hour before
they shot off yammering
to lord it at the tip.

big hoody
ugly bird
came down twice
sat square in the kitchen window
went caw caw
bashed his great horny beak twice hard
against the glass.

as if we were in an egg
big hoody was determined to smash.

but seems there's no omen in it.
hoodycrow's only

a bird
who's looking for a mate
and fallen for his own reflection

you know how people get.

III

mail comes
sometimes we send postcards
hope this finds you
we are much the same

midges very bad in evenings
we have woken every morning for a week
under the tin roof
listening to the rain
walking by the sea
we find clean bones
cork floats tiny
coral branches
green glass cockleshells
driftwood a broken
copper sprinkler rose gone green
and botched and oxidised
smooth pebbles mermaid purses
things to pick.
a collage on the windowledge.
I'd like
an art that could somehow marry
the washed-up manmade
and the wholly natural
make a change

don't even know
if I like cities or small places

heart urchin
rare to find an unbroken one

perfect from the sea
smaller
than a salt cellar
frail container
some marine-motif something
starlike etched on the shell
shake it you can tell
something small and dry and shrivelled is inside.

shake it and your page
is seasoned with smithereens of sand

heart urchin
something to hold in your hand.

Laundrette

We sit nebulous in steam.
It calms the air and makes the windows stream
rippling the hinterland's big houses to a blur
of bedsits – not a patch on what they were before.

We stuff the tub, jam money in the slot,
sit back on rickle chairs
not reading. The paperbacks in our pockets curl.
Our eyes are riveted. Our own colours whirl.

We pour in smithereens of soap. The machine sobs
through its cycle. The rhythm throbs
and changes. Suds drool and slobber in the churn.
Our duds don't know which way to turn.

The dark shoves one man in,
lugging a bundle like a wandering Jew. Linen
washed in public here.
We let out of the bag who we are.

This youngwife has a fine stack of sheets, each pair
a present. She admires their clean cut air
of colourschemes and being chosen. Are the dyes fast?
This christening lather will be the first test.

This woman is deadpan before the rinse and sluice
of the family in a bagwash. Let them stew in their juice
to a final fankle, twisted, wrung out into rope,
hard to unravel. She sees a kaleidoscope

for her to narrow her eyes and blow smoke at, his overalls
and pants ballooning, tangling with her smalls
and the teeshirts skinned from her wriggling son.
She has a weather eye for what might shrink or run.

This dour man does for himself. Before him,
half lost, his small possessions swim.
Cast off, random
they nose and nudge the porthole glass like flotsam.

The Bargain

The river in January is fast and high.
You and I
are off to the Barrows.
Gathering police-horses twitch and fret
at the Tron end of London Road and Gallowgate.
The early kick-off we forgot
has us, three thirty, rubbing the wrong way
against all the ugly losers
getting ready to let fly
where the two rivers meet.

January, and we're
looking back, looking forward,
don't know which way

but the boy
with three beautiful Bakelite
Bush radios for sale in Meadow's Minimarket is
buttonpopping stationhopping he
don't miss a beat   sings along   it's easy
to every changing tune,

Yes today we're in love aren't we?
with the whole splintering city
its big quick river   wintry bridges
its brazen black Victorian heart.
So what if every other tenement
wears its hearth on its gable end
all I want
is my glad eye to catch
a glint in your flinty Northern face again
just once. Oh I know it's cold
and coming down
and no we never lingered long among
the Shipbank traders.
Paddy's Market   underneath the arches

stank too much today
the usual wetdog reek rising
from piles of old damp clothes.

Somebody absolutely steamboats he says on
sweet warm wine
swigged plaincover from a paper bag
squats in a puddle with nothing to sell
but three bent forks   a torn
calendar (last year's)
and a broken plastic sandal.
So we hadn't the stomach for it today.
We don't deserve a bargain then!
No connoisseur can afford to be too scrupulous
about keeping his hands clean.
There was no doubt   the rare   the beautiful
and the bugle beaded   the real antique   dirt cheap
among the rags and drunks
you could easily take to the cleaners.

At the Barrows everything has its price
no haggling   believe me
this boy knows his radios.
Pure Utility
and what that's worth these days.
Suddenly the fifties are fashionable
and anything within a decade of art deco
a rarity you'll pay through the nose for.
The man with the patter and all these curtain lengths
in fibreglass is flabbergasted at the bargain
and says so in so many words.
Jesus, every other
arcade around here's
a 'Fire Surround Botique' –
and we watch the struggling families;
father carrying hearth home
mother wound up with kids.
All the couples we know fall apart
or have kids.

Oh we've never shouldered much.
We'll stick to small ikons for our home –
as long as they're portable –
a dartboard   a peacock feather
a stucco photoframe.

We queue in a blue haze of hot fat
for Danny's Do-Nuts that grit
our teeth with granules of sugar
I keep
losing you and finding you –
two stalls away you thumb
through a complete set of manuals for
primary teachers in the thirties
I rub my sleeve
on a dusty Chinese saucer
till the gilt shows through.
Oh come on   we promised
we'd not let our affection for the slightly cracked
trap us into such expenditure again.
Oh even if it is a bargain
we won't buy.
The stallholder says we'll be the death of her
she says   see January
it's been the doldrums the day.

And it's packing up time
with the dark coming early
and as cold as the river.
By the bus stop I show you
the beady bag and the maybe rosewood box
with the inlaid butterfly and the broken catch.
You've bought a record by the Shangri-las
a pin-stripe waistcoat that needs a stitch
it just won't get   and a book called 'Enquire
Within – Upon Everything'.

The raw cold gets colder.
There doesn't seem to be a lot to say.
I wish we could either mend things
or learn to throw them away.

In the Francis Bacon Room at the Tate

in every picture
   every figure
(except
the figure of Van Gogh
in Francis Bacon's 1957
Study for a Portrait)
has a defined space he must inhabit.

Delineate.
Cold steel. Prosthetic.
Chromium or crowbar.
Hotelroom neutral gloss over
suffering, over violence and loss.
Solid, marginally shifting walls enclose
all flesh.
Genitals, a curled rose.
Face a blur.
One limb a mere
stump. Gouge that tongue
plush soft and scarlet in its cage of teeth.
Look, where that knife-edged
shank-bone sinks beneath
that surface, is it ankle-deep
in fur rug
or barbed wire? Can't shrug
off normality, its terrible textures.
These pictures
bring it all home.
Every solitary figure is a loner.
Every smart pad frames its owner.

In the Francis Bacon Room at the Tate,
in every picture,
   every figure
(except
the figure of Van Gogh in Bacon's

1957 Study for a Portrait)
has this boxed-in space he must inhabit.

But Van Gogh
is a figure in a landscape that bleeds
on all sides from the picture edge,
flows from him all ways,
harshened under cruel sun
to acid scarlet and poison green.
Van Gogh is lonely, lumpen, out-of-place
being at one with the landscape.
He's rooted like an awkward tree,
tied to his own shadow, a black hole.
All there is to hem him is his hat
a slashed arc, burnt gold, sharp citrus.
Careful, it's a hat and not a halo.
And it offers not much shadow.
The only space Van Gogh has to inhabit
is this terrible landscape,
is the space beneath his hat.

Memo For Spring (1972)

Portrait of Liz Lochhead by Alasdair Gray.

Revelation

I remember once being shown the black bull
when a child at the farm for eggs and milk.
They called him Bob – as though perhaps
you could reduce a monster
with the charm of a friendly name.
At the threshold of his outhouse, someone
held my hand and let me peer inside.
At first, only black
and the hot reek of him. Then he was immense,
his edges merging with the darkness, just
a big bulk and a roar to be really scared of,
a trampling, and a clanking tense with the chain's jerk.
His eyes swivelled in the great wedge of his tossed head.
He roared his rage. His nostrils gaped like wounds.

And in the yard outside,
oblivious hens picked their way about.
The faint and rather festive jingling
behind the mellow stone and hasp was all they knew
of that Black Mass, straining at his chains.
I had always half-known he existed –
this antidote and Anti-Christ his anarchy
threatening the eggs, well rounded, self-contained –
and the placidity of milk.

I ran, my pigtails thumping on my back in fear,
past the big boys in the farm lane
who pulled the wings from butterflies and
blew up frogs with straws.
Past thorned hedge and harried nest,
scared of the eggs shattering –
only my small and shaking hand on the jug's rim
in case the milk should spill.

Poem for Other Poor Fools

Since you went I've only cried twice.
Oh never over you. Once
it was an old head at a bus window
and a waving hand.
Someone's granny, a careful clutcher of her handbag
and wearing a rainhat despite the fact
it wasn't raining. Yet
waving, waving to grandchildren already turned away
engrossed in sweets she had left them.
Old head. Waving hand.

Oh she wasn't the type to expose herself
to the vagaries of weather
(a rainhat in no rain)
Yet waving, waving to those who had already
turned away.

Then once it was a beggar by the pub doorway
and his naked foot.
Some drunk old tramp,
player of an out of tune mouthorgan
and begging. Instead of his cap,
his boot for alms.
His playing was hopeless,
his foot bare in the gutter in the rain,
his big boot before him, empty, begging.
Oh it was a scream. I laughed
and laughed till I cried.

It was just his poor
pink and purple naked foot
out on a limb
exposed.
And how (his empty boot) he got nothing
in return.

How Have I Been

since you last saw me?
Well,
I've never been lonely
I've danced at parties,
and drunk flat beer
with other men;
I've been to the cinema and seen
one or two films you would have liked
with other men;
I've passed the time in amusement arcades
and had one or two pretty fruitless
go'es on the fruit machine;
I've memorised the patterns
of miscellaneous neckties.
Indifferent, I
put varying amounts of sugar
in different coffee cups
and adjusted myself to divers heights
of assorted goodnight kisses, but
my breasts (once bitten)
shy away from contact
I keep a curb
on mind and body –
Love? I'm no longer
exposing myself.

On Midsummer Common

On midsummer common
it's too good to be true,
backdrop of cricketers,
punts on the river,
the champ of horses
and mayflies in June
mere midsummer commonplace.

Not in midsummer,
but with the real rain of more normal weather
putting a different slant on things,
my hard edged steel town
seen through the blur of bus windows.
Saturday afternoon streets crammed
with shoppers laden under leaden skies.
Out of the constant comedown of the rain, old men
in the final comedown of old age
file into public libraries to turn no pages.
Saturday. My town
can't contain itself.
Roars rise and fall,
stadiums spill
football crowds in columns
in the teeming rain.
Saturday buses are jampacked with football rowdies
all going over the score.
I am overlapped by all the fat and laughing losers
that pour from bingo parlours.
Outside cinemas, steadies
queue steadily to buy
their darkness by the square foot.
The palais and troc are choc-full
of gaudy girls dressed parrot fashion.
Saturday's all
social clubs, singers, swilled ale.
So much is spilt –

the steel clang, the clash of creeds,
the overflow of shouts and songs,
the sprawl of litter,
the seep of smells,
the sweat, the vinegar, the beer –
so much slops
into that night nothing goes gentle into,
not even rain.
Such a town
I feel at home to be at odds with.

Here on midsummer common
on a midsummer Saturday
you, this day, this place and I
are just exchanging pleasantries.
Oh, it's nice here, but
slagheaps and steelworks
hem my horizons
and something compels
me forge my ironies from a steel town.

Fragmentary

Twilight (six o'clock and
undrawn curtains). It's as if
upstairs
from me
lives some crazy projectionist
running all his reels at once.
Pub-sign neon scrawls credits on the sky that's
cinemascope for him. He
treats me to so many
simultaneous
home movies, situation comedies, kitchen sink dramas
I can't make sense of them –
just snippets, snatches with the sound gone,
mouthings in a goldfish bowl.

The Visit

We did not really want to go,
not very much,
but he said it was our Christian Duty
and anyway he had already booked the bus.
So we went
despite ourselves
dreading, half hoping to be horrified.
Through corridors with a smell,
bile greenish-yellow unfamiliar smell
of nothing *we* knew,
but of oldness, madness, blankness,
apathy and disinfectant.
We grinned.
We did not know what else to do.
A grimace of goodwill and Christian greetings,
hymn books clutched in sweaty palms.
We are the Church Youth Club to sing to you,
bring you the joy we have never felt.
We passed on through the strange men –
complex simple faces
so full of blankness you would not believe it –
bowing, smiling, nodding they ignored us,
or acknowledged us with sullen stares.
A tall orderly came towards us
with eyes that couldn't keep still
and a nervous twitch.
I wonder had he always been like that,
the watcher, the keeper-
calm of what prowled his cage?
We sang. The minister shut his eyes
and prayed from unironic lips
with easy phrases.

For me, only an orderly
who prayed with his eyes skinned.
Just the flick of eyes
which *can't* be everywhere at once.

After a Warrant Sale

I watched her go,
Ann-next-door
(dry eyed,
as dignified
as could be expected)
the day after they came,
sheriff court men
with the politeness of strangers
impersonally
to rip her home apart –
to tear her life along the dotted line
officially.

On the sideboard that went for fifteen bob,
a photograph.
Wedding-day Walter and
Ann: her hair was lightened,
and heart, with hopes.
No-one really knows
when it began to show –
trouble, dark roots.

It was common knowledge
there were faults on both sides,
and the blame –
whether it was over drink
or debt no-one seems to know,
or what was owing to exactly whom.
Just in the end the warrant sale
and Ann's leaving.

But what seemed strange:
I wondered why,
having stayed long past the death of love
and the ashes of hope,
why pack it up and go

over some sticks of furniture
and the loss of one's only partially
paid-for washing machine?

Those who are older tell me,
after a married year or two
the comforts start to matter
more than the comforting.
But I am very young,
expecting not too much of love –
just that it should completely solve me.
And I can't understand.

Phoenix

When crowsfeet get a grip on me
I'll call them laughter lines
I'll think of burnt-out romances
as being my old flames.

Daft Annie on Our Village Mainstreet

Annie
with your euphemisms to clothe you
with your not all there
    your sixpence short in the shilling
with your screw loose
    your crazy tick tock in the head
    your lurching pendulum
                slightly unbalanced
with your plimsolls in winter
with your big-boots in summer and
    your own particular unseasonal
    your unpredictable weather.

Annie
out of the mainstream
mainstreet Annie
down at the cross
with your religious mania
singing Salvation Army choruses
to all on Sunday.
Annie
with your unique place
    your pride of place
    in the community –
how
    to every village
    its doctor and its dominie
    its idiot.

Annie
with the village kids afraid of you
with your myth of witchery
with your mystery
    your big raw bones
and your hamfisted face.
with your touching every lamp-post

your careful measured paces down mainstreet
clothed in euphemisms
and epithets.
Daft Annie
your epitaph.

Obituary

We two in W2
walking,
and all the W2 ladies, their
hair coiffed and corrugated come
with well-done faces
from the hairdressers.
We together
laughing,
in our snobbery of lovers,
at their narrow vowels
and strange permed poodles.
Locked too long in love, our eyes
were unaccustomed to the commonplace.
        Seems silly now really.

We two in W2
walking
down Byres Road
passing unconcerned
a whole florist's
full of funerals,
the nightmare butcher's shop's
unnumbered horrors,
the hung fowls
and the cold fish
dead on the slab.
We saw ourselves duplicated
by the dozen in the chainstore
with no crisis of identity.
Headlines on newsagent's placards
caused us no alarm
Sandwichman's prophecies of doom
just slid off our backs.
The television showroom's window
showed us cities burning
in black and white but we

had no flicker of interest.
An ambulance charged screaming past
but all we noticed was the funny old
Saturday street musician.
          seems silly now really.

We two one Sunday
at the art galleries
looking only at each other.
We two one Sunday
in the museum –
wondering why the ownership of a famous man
should make a simple object a museum piece –
and I afraid
to tell you how
sometimes I did not wash your coffee cup for days
or touched the books you lent me
when I did not want to read.
Well, even at the time
          that seemed a bit silly really.

Christmas found me
with other fond and foolish girls
at the menswear counters
shopping for the ties that bind.
March found me
guilty of too much hope.
          seems silly now really.

Morning After

Sad how
Sunday morning finds us
separate after all,
side by side with nothing between us
but the Sunday papers.
Held like screens before us.
  Me, the Mirror
reflecting only on your closed profile.
  You, the Observer
encompassing larger, other issues.
Without looking up
you ask me please to pass the colour section.
I shiver
while you flick too quickly
        too casually through the pages, with
        too passing
        an interest.

Inventory

you left me
nothing but nail
parings orange peel
empty nutshells half filled
ashtrays dirty
cups with dregs of
nightcaps an odd hair
or two of yours on my
comb gap toothed
bookshelves and a
you shaped
depression in my pillow.

Grandfather's Room

In your room in the clutter of pattern
you lie.
Sunlight strains through lace curtains,
makes shadow patterns
on wallpaper's faded trellises,
on fat paisley cushions,
on the gingham table-cloth.
On the carpet, rugs
layer on layer like the years,
pattern on pattern,
cover the barest patches.
Geometric, floral, hand-made rag rugs,
an odd bit left over from the neighbours'
new stair carpet –
patterns all familiar
from other people's houses,
other people's lives.

In a clutter of patterns
you lie,
your shrunken head, frail
as a shell or a bird skull,
peeps from the crazy-paved
patch-work quilt.

Above your bed
in his framed death, your son,
my Uncle Robert that I never knew.
They say
he was well-known for his singing at weddings
and was a real nice lad, killed
in the war at twenty-one.
His photo, hung so long in the same place, has
merged with the wallpaper,
faded into the pattern.
(But it can't be moved now,

it has left its mark.)
Uncle Robert in a uniform
above your bedside table-top, the
medicines, the bright and bullet-shaped pills,
nothing in the angle of his smile
nor in the precise tilt of his cap, hinting
how soon, how suddenly he was to die.

There he is in black and white, believable.
Oh yes, he smiled and sang.
His sudden death stopped short
a slower certain dying, change.
While the other wall holds up
a scrap of nineteen thirty three,
maintains it's true.
A photo of the family (or so they say) –
that flop-haired boy my balding father?
and you, grandfather, tall and strong.
smouldering in a landscape of shut pits and silent chimneys?
It's framed like a fact,
set fair and square but has less weight
is less real
than those faint patterns traced
by a weak sun through lace curtains.
Pale shadows, constantly changing.

For my Grandmother Knitting

There is no need they say
but the needles still move
their rhythms in the working of your hands
as easily
as if your hands
were once again those sure and skilful hands
of the fisher-girl.

You are old now
and your grasp of things is not so good
but master of your moments then
deft and swift
you slit the still-ticking quick silver fish.
Hard work it was too
of necessity.

But now they say there is no need
as the needles move
in the working of your hands
once the hands of the bride
with the hand-span waist
once the hands of the miner's wife
who scrubbed his back
in a tin bath by the coal fire
once the hands of the mother
of six who made do and mended
scraped and slaved slapped sometimes
when necessary.

But now they say there is no need
the kids they say grandma
have too much already
more than they can wear
too many scarves and cardigans –
gran you do too much
there's no necessity.

At your window you wave
them goodbye Sunday.
With your painful hands
big on shrunken wrists.
Swollen-jointed. Red. Arthritic. Old.
But the needles still move
their rhythms in the working of your hands
easily
as if your hands remembered
of their own accord the pattern
as if your hands had forgotten
how to stop.

Something I'm Not

familiar with, the tune
of their talking, comes tumbling before them
down the stairs which (oh I forgot) it was my turn
to do again this week.
My neighbour and my neighbour's child. I nod, we're not
on speaking terms exactly.

I don't know much about her. Her dinners smell
different. Her husband's a busdriver,
so I believe.
She carries home her groceries in Grandfare bags
though I've seen her once or twice around the corner
at Shastri's for spices and such.
(I always shop there – he's open till all hours
making good.) How does she feel?
Her children grow up with foreign accents,
swearing in fluent Glaswegian. Her face
is sullen. Her coat is drab plaid, hides
but for a hint at the hem, her sari's
gold embroidered gorgeousness. She has
a jewel in her nostril.
The golden hands with the almond nails
that push the pram turn blue
in this city's cold climate.

Poem on a Day Trip

It's nice to go to Edinburgh.
Take the train in the opposite direction.
Passing through a hard land, a pitted
and pockmarked, slag-scarred, scraped land.
Coal. Colossus of pit-bings,
and the stubborn moors where Covenanters died.
Hartwood, Shotts, Fauldhouse, Breich –
something stirs me here
where the green veneer is thin,
the black-gut and the quarried ash-red
show in the gashes.
But the land changes
somewhere in the region of West and Mid Calder,
greener and gentler, rolling Lothians.
Edinburgh. Your names are grander –
Waverley, Newington, Corstorphine,
never Cowcaddens, Hillhead or Partick.
No mean city,
but genteel, grey and clean city
you diminish me –
make me feel my coat is cheap,
shabby, vulgar-coloured.
You make me aware of your architecture,
conscious of history and the way it has
of imposing itself upon people.
Princes Street.
I rush for Woolworth's anonymous aisles,
I feel at home here
you could be anywhere –
even in Glasgow

Overheard by a Young Waitress

Three thirty-fivish women met one day,
each well glossed against the others' sharp eyes for flaws.
Old school friends apparently – they slipped
with ease into the former conspiracy of dormitories,
and discussed over coffee and saccharine, the grounds
for divorce. All agreed love made
excessive demands on them,
wondered how long it must be missing
before it could be
Presumed Dead.

Notes on the Inadequacy of a Sketch

at Millport Cathedral, March 1970

Fields strung out so, piece-
meal on a crude felt-tip line
in real life revealed ribs
where the plough had skinned them alive.
My scrawl took the edge off the dyke.
Sure. But omitted to mark how
it held together, the gravity
of the situation (it being
a huddle of rough stone forms in a cold climate)
how it was set to hump across hills, or at what
intervals over which stones exactly
snails had scribbled silver.
I jotted down how fence
squared up to dyke (but nothing of
the wool tufts caught on random barbs)
how it bordered on that
ridiculous scrap of grass
(but failed to record its precise
and peculiarly Scottish green).
I made a sheer facade
of the cruciform cathedral, stated
only that the rectory garden
slanted towards an empty greenhouse
on the graveyard's edge.
For gravestones, I set mere slabs right-
angling to a surface I took at face value.
(I did not explain how at my feet
sprawled a rickle of rabbit bones
ribcage and spine in splinters,
skull intact.) I probed no roots.
I did not trace either gravestones'
legends or their moss (it let me read
between the lines the stones' survivals).
I selected what seemed to be essentials.
Here, where wind and rain

made a scapegoat of a scarecrow, my pen
took it for an easy symbol. But it's plain
setting down in black and white
wasn't enough, nor underlining
certain subtleties. This sketch became
a simile at best. It's no metaphor.
It says *under prevailing conditions*
smoke from a damp bonfire was
equal to tonal value to the sea.
So what?
                Today on the empty
summer's sand the March rain needled no-one.
(My sketch mentions no rain
neither how wet it was nor how straight
it fell nor that seagulls tried to call a halt
to it.) From my quick calligraphy of trees
no real loud rooks catcall the sea's
cold summersalt.

Letter from New England

from a small town, Massachusetts

I sip my coke at the counter
of the Osterville soda-fountain
that is also the Osterville news-stand, &
I watch Nothing Happening
out on mainstreet
of this small New England town.

just
the sun &
white clapboard houses with trees in between, &
certain cottonclad &
conservative spinsters nod at nodding acquaintances, &
occasional rocking chairs nod on front porches &
old men in panamas hail each other loudly, &
mothers compare feeding methods, &
the parson posts a letter &
some highschool kids are perched on the fence
    of the Pilgrim Fathers' Museum
    (open only on Sundays)
    practising real hard at sitting on fences so
    as to grow up to be
    realgood New Englanders, &
cars purr past, each containing
    one pale lady in sunglasses
    behind a smoke-tinted windscreen
    in transit between
    Ideal Home
    and beautyparlour, &
what-looks-to-me like a farmer
    puts a Big Box
    in the back of a Ford, &
my-bike-without-a-padlock
    sits for hours outside the library
    because you can Sorta Trust Folk
    in a small New England town

where no-one locks their doors.

business is slow, says the soda-jerk,
like molasses in janu-werry, &
I buy myself a *New York Times*
at the Osterville news-stand
(that is also the soda-fountain)
just to remind me that
This is America, &
America has Problems,
pollution &
recession &
escalation &
de-escalation &
women's liberation &
racial integration
which
is not-to-speak-of Unspeakable Problems like
Spiro T. Agnew
& not-to-mention Problems
like odorforming bacteria & horrid
halitosis
which as each &
every ad would warn us are
ever-ready to engulf us.

& I feel I should be somewhere Else
like
a be-in, or
a love-in, or
learning how the American Election System works, &
How To Make A President &
what *is* the difference between a
republican & a
dem-o-crat?

I should be
spectating at a looting, or
sightseeing in some ghetto, or

marching civil-righteously, or
rioting on campus &
striking matches
for people burning draftcards &
sticking pink bubblegum
on every seat in the senate
as a last-ditch attempt
at Nonviolent Action, or
out in California
getting genned-up generally
on the Voice of Youth's current (& ∴ correct)
Attitudes
to the kinds of Grass & Peace & Love
different from the grass & peace
you get for free in New England with
No Attitudes Necessary.

I should be somewhere else –
not
practising Non Involvement
(& taking a slow suntan)
eavesdropping on the Silent Majority
(& eating hot butterscotch &
ice cream sundae
with marshmallow sauce vanilla
cream and double nuts)
at the Osterville soda-fountain
that is also the news-stand
in this small New England town.

Getting Back

I was to ring you, remember,
the minute I got back. (Your number
among all those American addresses that came since.)
        I look
it up where you wrote it, something special in my book.
Four months. Four thousand miles apart and more.
        Keeping in touch
with us both on the move and all, no fixed addresses,
        was too much
to ask of us. From the Acropolis to the Empire State
it's a far cry. Then, between San Francisco and
        Istanbul, late
August burned and the distance grew.
That close and now at odds. You
had done with the sun by the time I got round to it.
You woke up, I sank into sleep, worlds away. We moved
        in opposite
directions in the dark about each other's days.
Now, I only lift the telephone and the operator says
she's trying to connect us. Between us four miles,
        no distance,
it's a local call – I should get through for sixpence.

But I just got back. No small change. I forgot
to check on it. I push a quarter in the shilling slot,
pips stop (my heartbeat), you reply to my
        small and civic dishonesty.
I jingle my pocket – nickles, dimes,
        meaningless currency –
and try to picture you at the receiving end – moustache
        at the mouth-piece
unless you've changed a lot. I take a breath
        'And how was Greece?'
We namedrop cities into silences, feel the distance grow
find no common ground to get back to. I know
in my bones, nothing's the same anymore.
Don't you remember the girl I'm a dead ringer for?

Box Room

First the welcoming. Smiles all round. A space
for handshakes. Then she put me in my place –
oh, with concern for my comfort. 'This room
was always his – when he comes home
it's here for him. Unless of course,' she said,
'He brings a Friend.' She smiled. 'I hope the bed
is soft enough? He'll make do tonight
in the lounge on the put-u-up. All right
for a night or two. Once or twice before
he's slept there. It'll all be fine I'm sure –
next door if you want to wash your face.'
Leaving me 'peace to unpack' she goes. My weekend case
(lightweight, glossy, made of some synthetic
miracle) and I are left alone in her pathetic
shrine to your lost boyhood. She must
think she can brush off time with dust
from model aeroplanes. I laugh it off in self defence,
who have come for a weekend to state my permanence.

Peace to unpack – but I found none
in this spare room which once contained you. (Dun-
coloured walls, one small window which used to frame
your old horizons.) What can I blame
for my unrest, insomnia? Persistent fear
elbows me, embedded deeply here
in an outgrown bed. (Narrow, but no narrower
than the single bed we sometimes share.)
On every side you grin gilt edged from long-discarded selves
(but where do I fit into the picture?) Your bookshelves
are crowded with previous prizes, a selection
of plots grown thin. Your egg collection
shatters me – that now you have no interest
in. (You just took one from each, you never wrecked a nest,

you said.) Invited guest among abandoned objects,
   my position
is precarious, closeted so – it's dark, your past a premonition
I can't close my eyes to. I shiver despite
the electric blanket and the deceptive mildness of the night.

Song for Coming Home

I browsed among the dress shop windows
(The town, the sun, the styles were new.)
I was looking for something lightweight for summer
And picked on you.

But what was less than love in summer
Autumn turned to almost hate.
So now I leave our bed of roses
With a hurt like a heavy weight.

I'm drinking beer in a speeding buffet
Along with some soldier I've met on this train.
My father will pick me up at the station
But I'll have to put me together again.

George Square

George Square
idleness
an island
children splashing
in a sea of pigeons
pigeons strutting
pigeon-toed.

And we
city dwellers
sitting
separate
close together.
City dwellers
we only know
nature captive –
zoos and gardens
Latin-tagged.
We know no earth
or roots.
We see no slow
season shift
but sudden summer
blaze a concrete day
and catch us unawares.
We can find no sense
in traffic lights'
continual change of emphasis.

Nature captive:
this is a city
nature's barred.
But the flowers
bound and bedded
bloom
incurable as cancer

and as for fat old ladies'
flowery
summer dresses
my god they really are
a riot.

Man on a Bench

This old man
has grown year-weary
no joy in changing seasons, just
another blooming spring
another sodden summer
another corny old autumn
and another winter
to leave him cold.

Carnival

Glass roof holds down a
stale air of excitement,
bottles up noise.
It's all screams and legs
cutting prescribed arcs. We walk,
the lights revolve around you.
People spin at tangents,
swing limit-wards on chain end.
Collisions are less than inevitable.

The speedway is a whirlpool.
The waltzer reels out-of-time
to ten popsongs.
Pressures force skirts up, girls bare
their teeth and scream.
You say it's screams of pleasure.
The timid roll pennies.

Aunt Sally has ten men. They
grin and shake their heads. I
miss the point.
The hall of mirrors hints at all sorts
of horrible distortions, but
you're favourably reflected in my eyes.
We play the fruit machines.

I spin to a mere blur on a wheelspoke
about your axis. There is a smell of onions
and axle grease.
The ghost train has pop-up fears for fun,
makes me laugh off mine and try
octopus, big dipper, roller coaster.
(Single riders pay double fare.)

Here is no plain sailing, all bump
and jerk. Above the screams, the sound

of some clown laughing.
Showmen shuffle hoops, push darts.
Prizes are sheer trash, and every lady wins.
You buy me candyfloss and smile.
I sink my teeth into sweet damn all.

Cloakroom

Firstly
you girls who are younger
and therefore more hopeful,
thinking this is Woman's Own World
and that a dab of such and such
perfume behind the ears
will lure
a kid-gloved
dream lover
who knows how to treat a girl
gently.
You think you can tangle him in your curls
and snare him with your fishnet
stockings.

Secondly
we girls who are older
and therefore – but *is* it wiser
to recognise our failure
reflected in succeeding Saturday nights?
Our eyes are blank
of illusions
but we automatically
lengthen lashes, lacquer hair
lipstick our lips for later
and the too easily faked closeness
of close-mouth kisses
which always
leave a lot to be desired.

The Choosing

We were first equal Mary and I
with same coloured ribbons in mouse-coloured hair
and with equal shyness,
we curtseyed to the lady councillor
for copies of Collins' Children's Classics.
First equal, equally proud.

Best friends too Mary and I
a common bond in being cleverest (equal)
in our small school's small class.
I remember
the competition for top desk
at school service.
And my terrible fear
of her superiority at sums.

I remember the housing scheme
where we both stayed.
The same houses, different homes,
where the choices were made.

I don't know exactly why they moved,
but anyway they went.
Something about a three-apartment
and a cheaper rent.
But from the top deck of the high-school bus
I'd glimpse among the others on the corner
Mary's father, mufflered, contrasting strangely
with the elegant greyhounds by his side.
He didn't believe in high school education,
especially for girls,
or in forking out for uniforms.

Ten years later on a Saturday –
I am coming from the library –
sitting near me on the bus,

Mary
with a husband who is tall,
curly haired, has eyes
for no one else but Mary.
Her arms are round the full-shaped vase
that is her body.
Oh, you can see where the attraction lies
in Mary's life –
not that I envy her, really.

And I am coming from the library
with my arms full of books.
I think of those prizes that were ours for the taking
and wonder when the choices got made
we don't remember making.

Homilies from Hospital

There was a bit of an upset
one afternoon. Well, waking
from an after-dinner nap (you get so tired) I
heard sounds, moans I suppose you would call them,
small cries, a kind of
whimpering.
That Miss Galbraith   it was her all right.
The curtains were well-drawn but
hanging down
below their floral edge (they're no longer than bed-level)
her half
            -leg cut off just below the knee
and a nurse with forceps or something
at the stitches.
It was loose
around the bonestump, like leather folded under, gathered and
hamstrung with catgut.
The skin was a bit on the blue side, oh
                                                  her
                                                  shrieks   and   three
loud dark drops of bad blood
from where the clean thing had probed it.
Of course all this was none
too pleasant
for anyone concerned. But on the whole here
it's a well-ordered existence.
Daily
those of us who are up to it, fix the flowers.
(daffodils are in season   make a fine show for
the visiting hour).
There's not much to it to tell the truth
it's just a matter of the fresh ones
arranging them as best you can and
picking out the dead ones
then disposing of them in the polythene sack in the slunge
which smells a bit.

This is only natural.

I had my dressing changed today.
To be honest I had not thought to be flawed
so very visibly.
But when all is said and done, no matter.
Getting better is the main thing.

Up and about again. The world
shrinks to the size of the ward
and this dull day room.
Weak sun and one day much like
any other. We are on christian name terms
in no time.
Newspapers come, full of nonsense
BLIND CLIMBING ACE TO WED
EX-ORANGE CHIEF ACCUSED.
We are recovering.
You could call this a breathing space,
a chance to catch up on last Christmas's
correspondence.

But for the most part
looking out of the window
at the stray sheep in the hospital grounds
making themselves ill
silly creatures
cropping in the rhubarb patch, is about all we are good for.
We all agree operations
fairly take it out of you.
There is a TV we don't watch much.
We cannot laugh / we are in stitches.
The way we feel
a sneeze would split us at the seam.   Oh,
but our wounds won't gape unless we are unwise &
overdo things.
We are reminded healing hurts.
We all have wounds
                                        which will

get better through time, the marks
fade into ferns like fossils.
become old wounds.
All in all most of us are making good
recoveries. With luck we'll be home soon,
back to our loved ones
(oh and here's hoping)
because they love us they will also
love our scars.

Object

I, love,
am capable of being looked at
from many different angles. This
is your problem.
In this cold north light it may
seem clear enough.
You pick your point of view
and stick to it, not veering much –
this
being the only way to make any sense of me
as a formal object. Still
I do not relish it, being
stated so – my edges defined
elsewhere than I'd imagined them
with a crispness I do not possess.

The economy of your line does not spare me
by its hairsbreadth.
I am limited. In whose likeness
do you reassemble me?
It's a fixed attitude you
force me into.
Cramp knots calf muscles;
pins and needles rankle in my arm;
my shoulder aches;
irked, I am aware of my extremities.
A casual pose, at first it seemed
quite natural. My features freeze.
A snapshot's decision would have demanded nothing
much of me in the way of endurance.
Perhaps your eye's lens, being selective, is more merciful?
It flicks
constantly between us, taking stock,
trying to see me in proper proportion.
I did not choose which face to confront you with.

As a diversion
my eyes are allowed just this
wedge of studio and window space
over your left shoulder
and above your head.

Over and over, indifferent,
my boredom records it, raw and formless,
studio clutter
the floorboards irregularities
a knot or two
occasional splinters going against the grain;
Random spatters on the white wall –
cerulean, terre verte,
transparent golden ochre; black
dust on white ledge; chestnut tree's topmost
pale candles flickering beyond the sill,
cutting the clean edge of the attic opposite;
(once, over there, mirrored,
seen at several removes if I strained my eyes enough,
a woman in an overall
entering that dim room and
later leaving again, shutting out a square of light).
the thin wisps of smoke from those strange-shaped
chimney pots, the innumerable tones of grey
and green-grey merging, Spring glimmering.

In this view of things
too much to take into account is what it amounts to:
But you, love,
set me down in black and white exactly.
I am at once
reduced and made more of.

Wedding March

Could I buy a white dress and hope for good weather?
Could I take something borrowed? Could we bind us together?
And while Visions of Sugar Plums danced in each head,
could we lie long content on the bed that we'd made?

No, I've not my own house in order enough
to ever make you a tidy wife.
Could I learn to waste not
and want not –
make soup from bones,
save wool scraps, bake scones
from sour milk. Would I ask for more
than to lunch alone on what's left over from the night before?
Could I soothe our children's night time bad dream fear
with nursery rhymes, and never find my cupboard bare?
Imagine an old handbag full of photographs,
once in a blue moon I'd drag them out for laughs –
smiling at poses I once carefully arranged,
in hoots at the hemlines and how we've changed.

We'll try. It still is early days.
I'll try and mend my sluttish ways.
We'll give our kitchen a new look –
a lick of paint, a spice rack, and a recipe book.
I'll watch our tangled undies bleaching clean
in the humdrum of the laundromat machine.
I'll take my pet dog vacuum on its daily walk through rooms,
and knowing there is no clean sweep,
keep busy still with brooms.

Riddle-Me-Ree

My first is in life (not contained within heart)
My second's in whole but never in part.
My third's in forever, but also in vain.
My last's in ending, why not in pain?

is love the answer?

Memo to Myself for Spring

April
April first you must fool me
I am no longer
anybody's fool.
I have danced with too many
velvet tongued men.
I have seen too many
plaster effigies of saints
for faith to mean much.
Hope
is treacherous
and much to be guarded against in April.
I refuse to put out with
any more charity –
I won't be as mad as March in April.
April you confidence trickster,
you very practical
practical joker –
your clichéd burgeoning and budding
calculated
to set me wandering in a forest of cosmetic counters'
lyric poetry.
You urge me,
buy a lipstick
treat yourself to a new dress
try again.
But April first you must fool me.
April
I fear you
May